1947
GRACE HOPPER, a computer scientist and a US Navy admiral, popularizes the idea of programming languages and the term "debugging" for fixing computer problems.

1947
AILEEN HERNANDEZ graduates from Howard University, and by 1965 she is leading the newly formed EEOC (Equal Employment Opportunity Commission).

1957
BETTY FRIEDAN circulates a questionnaire to her college classmates, and the responses lead her to write the bestselling *The Feminine Mystique* and later to found the National Organization for Women (NOW).

1960
The thirteen women of the **MERCURY 13** prove that they are as capable of going into space as men.

1962
Vice president Lyndon Johnson effectively bans women from space by banning them from military combat, though the **MERCURY 13** had proved they were as capable of going into space as men.

1960
DIANE NASH and her peers successfully desegregate the Nashville, Tennessee, lunch counters, a turning point in the civil rights movement. Not long after, Nash and others cofound the Student Nonviolent Coordinating Committee.

1964
MARGARET CHASE SMITH, the first woman to serve in both houses of Congress, becomes the first woman nominated for the presidency at a major party's convention. She loses the Republican nomination but becomes the longest-serving female senator until Barbara Mikulski is sworn in for a fifth term in 2011.

1955
ROSA PARKS, a longtime civil rights activist, refuses to give up her bus seat to a white passenger, initiating the Montgomery bus boycott.

1961
Alan Shepard makes his inaugural trip into space. Though a computer processed the route, he personally asked **KATHERINE JOHNSON** to confirm it with her manual calculation. She was spot on!

1965
DUSTY ROADS, JEAN MONTAGUE, and other flight attendants arrive at the EEOC headquarters in Washington, DC, to file a complaint against the airlines for forcing women to retire at the age of thirty-two.

1958
Future Xerox CEO **URSULA BURNS** is born on the Lower East Side of Manhattan.

1963
DOROTHY HEIGHT, leader of the National Council of Negro Women and a close ally of First Lady Eleanor Roosevelt, is the only woman seated on the stage when Martin Luther King Jr. delivers his famous "I Have a Dream" speech.

1961
FANNIE LOU HAMER, one of the most vocal and active members of the Student Nonviolent Coordinating Committee, is admitted to the hospital for a tumor and is unknowingly sterilized—a procedure that makes it impossible for women to have children. In some cases, like Fannie Lou's, it has been done intentionally to reduce the number of black babies being born.

WE are MAKERS

REAL WOMEN AND GIRLS SHAPING OUR WORLD

A MAKERS BOOK

by

AMY RICHARDS

VIKING

VIKING

An imprint of Penguin Random House LLC, New York

First published in the United States of America by Viking, an imprint of Penguin Random House LLC, 2019

Visit us online at penguinrandomhouse.com

LIBRARY OF CONGRESS CATALOGING-IN-PUBLICATION DATA IS AVAILABLE.

ISBN 9780451468925 * Manufactured in China * Book design by Nancy Brennan * Text set in FreightText Pro

1 3 5 7 9 10 8 6 4 2

PHOTO CREDITS

All photos courtesy of MAKERS, except where noted below.

P. 10: NASA (Jemison, Johnson, Cobb); Library of Congress (O'Connor); courtesy of Ana Garcia (Garcia). P. 12: Library of Congress (O'Connor). P. 13: Collection of the Supreme Court of the United States (Ginsburg; Ginsburg, Sotomayer, Kagan). P. 15: by Bryce Kanights (Armanto). P. 17: by Sarinya Srisakul (FDNY). P. 18–19: NASA (Jemison, Cobb). P. 20: NASA (Johnson). P. 21: by Ariadne White, courtesy of Marin Alsop (Alsop). P. 22: Wikipedia/Senate Democrats (Senate women); Danica Racing, Inc. (Patrick); Wikimedia/Sara Melikian (Chu). P. 25: by PVAMU, Michael Thomas (Simmons); AP Photo/Ron Edmonds (signing). P. 27: Danica Racing, Inc. (Patrick). P. 28: by Larry Gordon (Gordon). P. 30: courtesy of Linda Alvarado (Alvarado). P. 32: Library of Congress (Obamas); Wikimedia/Cari Lender (Blume); Wikimedia/ by Alison Harbaugh for the Maryland Film Festival (Dunham); Wikimedia/Gage Skidmore (Cisneros); Wikimedia/Steve Jurvetson (Grandin). P. 38: Wikimedia/Susan Lesch (Catchings). P. 43: Wikimedia/Braedon Farr. P. 44: Wikimedia/Edwin Martinez (Williams); Wikimedia/ José Goulão (Keys); Wikimedia/Nancy Wong (Ferraro); Library of Congress/Maureen Keating (Clinton). P. 46: by Roger Prigent, courtesy of Diane von Furstenberg (von Furstenberg). P. 49: courtesy of Hillary Rodham Clinton (Clinton). P. 50: by Andrea Mohin/*The New York Times*/Redux (Ferraro). P. 52: Wikimedia/Kelly Bell Photography (Hirono). P. 53: by Noam Galai/WireImage (Cruz). P. 54: Wikimedia/ Edwin Martinez (Williams). P. 56: Wikimedia/Ted Eytan (Mock); *Boston Herald* (Switzer); courtesy of Girls Who Code 5th Anniversary Gala (Prabhu); Wikimedia/United States State Department (Kim). P. 60: © Annie Leibovitz (Copeland). P. 61: courtesy of LeanIn.org (Sandberg). P. 63: courtesy of Christy Haubegger (Haubegger). P. 65: Wikimedia/Juston Smith (Mock). P. 68: Wikimedia/Mobilus in Mobili (2018 Women's March); courtesy of Barbara Burns (Burns); © Annie Leibovitz (Steinem). P. 76: Wikimedia/VOA (2017 Women's March). P. 78: courtesy of Barbara Burns (Burns). P. 79: Library of Congress (ERA March). P. 80: Wikimedia/Alec Perkins (Saujani); Wikimedia/© Georgia Institute of Technology 2008/Rob Felt (Howard); by Bill Young/*San Francisco Chronicle*/Polaris (Hernandez); Library of Congress (Curie). P. 87: Library of Congress (Curie); by Bill Young/*San Francisco Chronicle*/Polaris (Hernandez). P. 88: Library of Congress (Friedan). P. 89: © Maya Lin Studio, courtesy Pace Gallery (Lin). P. 92: by Paul Morigi/Getty Images (Rice). P. 93: Wikimedia/WhiteHouse.gov/ Joyce N. Boghosian (Jarrett); Wikimedia/Kenneth C. Zirkel (Simmons). P. 94 : Wikimedia/*Ms.* magazine (Rhimes). P. 96: by Chris Lee @ christleephotonyc (Cowman and Miller); US Women's Basketball Team NBA Photos (Leslie); by Patrick P. Evenson/US Marine Corps (Wright); Wikimedia/ Stephanie Moreno (DuVernay). P. 98: Wikimedia/Gage Skidmore (Leslie). P. 100: by Grant Leighton, courtesy of Marin Alsop (Alsop). P. 101: by Caitlin Ochs (Cowman and Jordan).

The PBS Logo is a registered trademark of the Public Broadcasting Service and used with Permission.

Contents

What Is MAKERS?

by
DYLLAN McGEE

WHEN I WAS TWELVE years old, I wanted to be an actress. After I graduated from college, I got my first job in media, but it wasn't exactly what I thought it would be. I had wanted to be in front of the camera just like newscaster Katie Couric! After more than one person suggested I might be better behind the camera, I took the hint. Luckily, I soon found myself working for a documentary film company. I got to do a film about 9/11, one about Ted Kennedy, several about African American lives, and many others that I'm very proud of.

Around 2006, I started wondering about something: Where were the women? Were there any documentaries that looked at the women's movement? I found a few, but nothing comprehensive about contemporary women in America, so I got to work. First, I planned a film capturing the last fifty years or so of the women's movement in America. Once my colleagues and I started interviewing women, one three-hour film hardly seemed enough! How could I do justice to the vast number of women who changed the world you and I were born into? These women made it possible for others to be astronauts, firefighters, professional athletes, and more, and they deserved more screen time.

I decided to create a project to give these women the time they deserved, and I called it MAKERS—because a maker makes things happen, and all these women were certainly doing that. That was one of the project's main criteria for whom to include, and we also considered other questions, like: Which women were the first in their fields? Who were the worker bees, who maybe didn't get the full attention they deserved for changing the world for the better? Who was brave enough to dare to do something others hadn't? Who was breaking through barriers? Who was there at the turning points in history? I knew I couldn't do full justice to women's stories, but I could make a dent in what was pretty much an untold story.

Of course, I didn't do all of this by myself! I had a great partnership with PBS, which broadcast the first MAKERS film in 2013 and six others that came out a year later. The six additional films went into greater detail on some of the topics that needed more time. They were titled *Women in Comedy*, *Women in Hollywood*, *Women in Space*, *Women in War*, *Women in Business*, and *Women in Politics*. I was also lucky to get the support of AOL in building the world's largest online platform of women's stories. Plus, there were hundreds of filmmakers, editors, and producers who were enlisted to help. And of course there were the women who entrusted me with their stories.

Here's a wonderful thing about MAKERS: as much as it might seem that it's about inspiring others, its impact has also been very personal. In creating MAKERS, I realized how great it is to be a woman, and to be proud of that.

MAKERS continues to grow—more films, more women, and more inspiring stories. My greatest hope is that these stories will inspire and motivate you, and that you'll find a way to be a maker in your own life!

Introduction

by

AMY RICHARDS

HI! I'M AMY RICHARDS, the author of this book.

Many of the people in this book did amazing things, like run for president and travel to space. But when they were younger, they were just like you: young people with *big* dreams.

In these pages, you'll read about women who've influenced things you probably do every day, like play sports or use a computer. For example, Maria Pepe wasn't allowed to play in Little League, but she fought for the right of girls to be able to, and Reshma Saujani, founder of Girls Who Code, is helping girls all over the US learn how to code. Some stories might shock you, some might make you cry—but I guarantee that *all* of them will inspire you to achieve great things.

As I started watching the stories that MAKERS was gathering, I realized how many of us have common experiences, like being afraid of failure, being influenced by our family, and wanting to make the world a better place. So rather than organize this book chronologically or by jobs, I decided to weave it together around themes—like being the first to do something, standing up for what's right, and dreaming big. You might be surprised by how many of these themes you identify with!

You'll see that I tried to include as many voices as I could, whether they were famous people, like Oprah and Alicia Keys, or women you might never have heard of, like construction company owner Linda Alvarado or breakdancer Ana "Rokafella" Garcia. You'll also find information about important historical moments, and you'll hear about kids doing amazing things in the "Young & Bold" sections scattered throughout. And don't miss the "A Kid's Take" quotes from kids just like you who were inspired by the women in this book.

Note that the women included in this book are just a sampling of those featured on Makers.com and by no means make up a comprehensive view of all women who've had a big impact in our world. Still, in these pages, I hope you'll meet someone who comes from a similar background as you or has the same fears that you have (and has learned how to overcome them!), or that you discover a job you never knew existed. Most important, I hope you'll think differently about what you can—and *will*—achieve.

Happy reading!

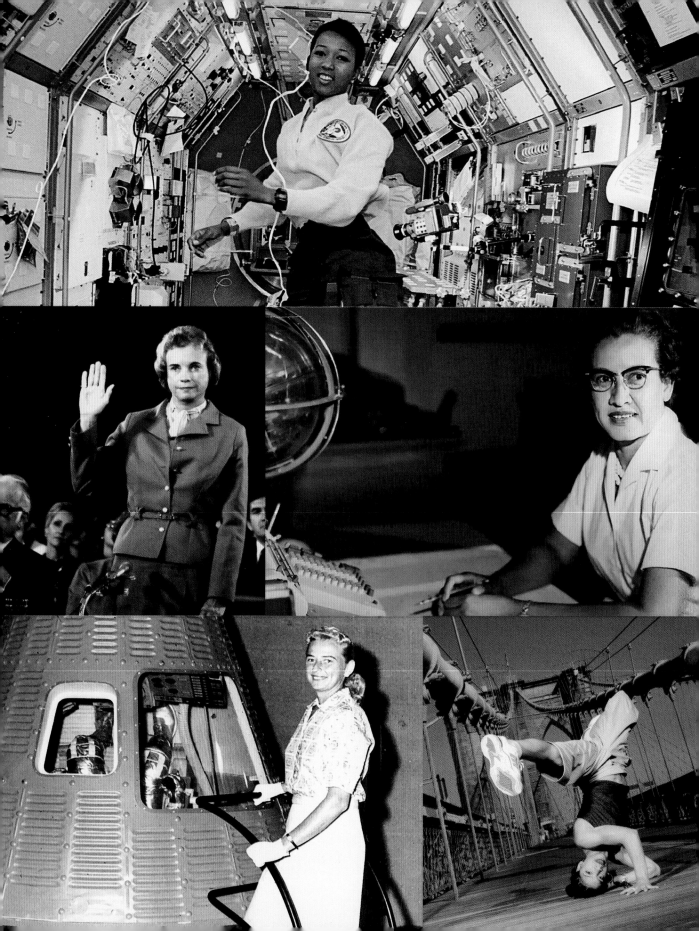

1

GIRLS CAN DO THAT!

"I really want to be a _____ when I grow up."

"What? You can't do that! You're a girl!"

EVER HAD THAT CONVERSATION? We hope not. We hope that you, and everyone you know, understand that no job or career is off-limits because of your gender.

But women in generations that have come before you were, well, not so lucky. Many of them had that kind of conversation all the time.

And they set out to change it.

In this chapter, we'll meet women who followed their dreams into professions that were dominated by men. In the 1950s, **Sandra Day O'Connor** was one of only three women in her law school class, but she eventually made history by being the first woman to join the United States Supreme Court. Decades later, **Ana "Rokafella" Garcia** was determined to make it in break-dancing even though it was considered a "guy's" dance style, and firefighter **Brenda Berkman** had to prove that, as

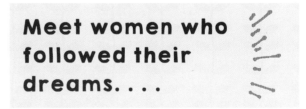

Meet women who followed their dreams. . . .

a woman, she was just as capable as a man. When **Mae Jemison** was a little girl, all astronauts who traveled into space were male—but that didn't stop her from wanting to go

Top: Mae Jemison; center, left: Sandra Day O'Connor; center, right: Katherine Johnson; bottom, left: Jerrie Cobb (Mercury 13); bottom, right: Ana "Rokafella" Garcia.

there someday. Fun fact: Hillary Clinton (read more about her in chapter 4) also wanted to become an astronaut. When she was sixteen years old, Hillary wrote to NASA (the National Aeronautics and Space Administration) about her plans. They wrote back and told her, "We don't take women."

These trailblazers pursued their passions, but it took persistence, and they didn't have many (or any!) female role models to inspire them. Read on and let their stories inspire *you*.

★ ★ ★ ★ ★

These days, we see women as lawyers on TV, in movies, in the news, and in our communities and families. But not too long ago, female lawyers were uncommon: in 1972, less than 10 percent of law school graduates were women. In 2017, that number was over 50 percent. Thumbs up for progress!

In the past, even if a woman was able to earn a law degree, she might still have had trouble getting work as an attorney. When former Supreme Court justice **Sandra Day O'Connor** graduated from Stanford Law School in 1952, she applied for dozens of jobs at law firms and was told over and over again, "We don't hire women."

Sandra didn't let those rejections steer her off course. She knew of a local attorney in San Mateo County, California, who'd once had a woman lawyer on his staff, and she approached him about a job. He wasn't thrilled with the idea at first, so Sandra wrote him a letter, convincing him to let her work for free until he was able to pay her. She remembers: "That was my first job as a lawyer. I worked for no salary, and I put my desk in with the secretary."

▷ WHAT DOES A SUPREME COURT JUSTICE DO?

The job of the US Supreme Court justices is to make sure new laws and lower court decisions follow the rules laid out in the Constitution. The Supreme Court receives many cases but doesn't handle and decide on (or, in legal-speak, "hear") all of them. Once cases are presented to the justices, they spend months deliberating—and not always agreeing on—a verdict. There are only two requirements for being a justice: you have to be nominated by the president of the United States and approved by the Senate Judiciary Committee.

Sandra did eventually get paid at that job. After years of hard work and time off to raise her three kids, Sandra was elected to the Arizona State Senate. She examined state laws that discriminated against women and eventually amended every single one—"amended" means "officially changed" in legal-speak—to make them fair for both genders.

In 1981, President Ronald Reagan appointed Sandra as the first female judge to the US Supreme Court, the country's highest federal court, where she served until her retirement in 2006. At that point, she shifted her focus to a new generation of leaders by creating an organization called iCivics, which makes video games to help kids learn how the government works. "My appointment just opened the doors," Sandra says. "And it was not only in the United States; it immediately had an effect in other parts of the world with other opportunities for women. It was quite amazing to see." By 2010, three of the nine justices on the Supreme Court were women: Sonia Sotomayor, Ruth Bader Ginsburg, and Elena Kagan.

* * * * *

Ruth Bader Ginsburg

Harvard Law School first admitted women in 1950, and by the mid-1950s Supreme Court justice **Ruth Bader Ginsburg** was one of them. She and the other nine women in her class (of five hundred!) were once invited to the dean's house for a "welcoming" dinner, which turned out to be not so welcoming for them. Ruth remembers: "After dinner, the dean brought us into his living room. He set up the chairs in a semicircle and called on each of us to tell him why we were at Harvard Law School occupying a seat that could be held by a man." What would you say if someone asked you a question like that?

Breakdancing

Breakdancing (or b-boying) is a style of street dance that started mostly with black and Puerto Rican youths in New York City in the 1980s. The dance quickly became popular worldwide. It consists of four basic movements: toprock (steps performed while standing), downrock (any movement on the floor with the hands supporting the dancer as much as the feet), power moves (acrobatic moves that require momentum, speed, endurance, and strength), and freezes (stylish poses that require the dancer to suspend him/herself off the ground using upper-body strength). The individual dancer varies and mixes up these steps however they want. Breakdancing is typically danced to hip-hop, funk, and breakbeats (electronic music and percussive rhythm).

While Sandra was making a difference in the courts, New Yorker **Ana "Rokafella" Garcia** was making headlines for her breakdancing.

Raised in East Harlem by Puerto Rican parents, Ana knew people had different expectations for her than they had for boys. "Being of Latino background, there was a difference between what the males could get away with and what the females had to do," she explains. But Ana's mother wanted more for her daughter. Ana remembers, "Without being so blatant about the women's movement, I think my mother was always letting me know that this is our time, and if we have a chance, take it."

Ana first saw boys breakdancing on the streets of New York City and decided to get serious about it in seventh grade after performing in a talent show. "That was my moment," she recalls. "As soon as I walked offstage I thought,

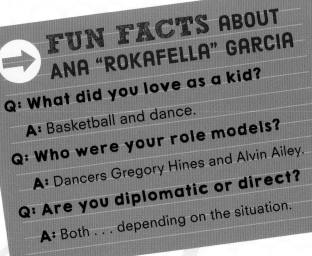

FUN FACTS ABOUT ANA "ROKAFELLA" GARCIA

Q: What did you love as a kid?

A: Basketball and dance.

Q: Who were your role models?

A: Dancers Gregory Hines and Alvin Ailey.

Q: Are you diplomatic or direct?

A: Both . . . depending on the situation.

Lizzie Armanto started skateboarding when she was fourteen years old. She's one of only twenty-five people in the world ever to have done a loop—a circle in the air! She won the World Cup Skateboarding's Ladies Bowl several times and has no plans of stopping—especially since skateboarding will debut in the 2020 Olympics. "When I see another [woman] do something, skating-wise, it pushes me more," says Lizzie. "In a sense, you can't be what you can't see. It's one less boundary you have to go through."

'Oh my god, I really want to do this!'" Have you had an OMG moment like that, when you discovered a passion?

Men dominated the hip-hop and breakdancing subcultures in the 1990s, but that didn't discourage Ana. "I really wanted to battle all the guys. I got skills, and the skills speak volumes," she says. Ana also wanted people to know that there's more to hip-hop

> **"I think my mother was always letting me know that this is our time, and if we have a chance, take it."**

than the "woman in a thong, shaking her butt" they might see in music videos. "A lot has changed," adds Ana. "There are way more b-girls now. Hip-hop is a culture. It's expression, it's freedom, and it's positive."

Ana eventually founded Full Circle, an organization that empowers young dancers through the positive power of hip-hop. She says, "I'm letting people know, you can be a woman and be a badass breaker. When you see me, you're seeing excellence, and men don't have a hold on the word 'excellence.'"

* * * * *

In 1982, when Ana "Rokafella" Garcia was just a kid, **Brenda Berkman** became one of the first woman firefighters hired by the New York City Fire Department.

Brenda was raised in a suburb of Minneapolis, Minnesota. She grew up with the belief that women could become teachers, nurses, or secretaries, but once they became mothers, they should stay at home and raise their children. What do *you* think about that idea?

As a young adult, Brenda knew she wanted to help people. While she was finishing law school at New York University, she thought: *Who do people call when they need help? Firefighters!* At the time, there weren't any woman firefighters in the New York City Fire Department, but Brenda was determined to become one anyway.

Like all firefighter candidates, she had to undergo a physical test, which had recently been made tougher. Brenda felt this new test was designed specifically to discriminate against women. For instance, the test required you to fling a 120-pound duffel bag over your shoulder and run up three flights of stairs with it to simulate the rescue of a person from a burning building. But Brenda knew that firefighters were actually trained to rescue people by dragging them out and down, since heat and smoke rise. She filed a federal sex discrimination suit against the NYC Fire Department in 1977 that challenged the fairness and relevance of the test. Brenda won the case. Soon she and forty-one other women took the new test, passed it, and became NYC's first female firefighters!

→ **A KID'S TAKE**

"Brenda Berkman is so brave! After hearing her story, I was thrilled that even though she was harassed, she still didn't give up. I kept thinking that she can do anything she put her mind to." —Isatou Bah, age 14

Still, many of Brenda's male coworkers didn't make her job easy. They made death threats against her, refused to talk or eat with her at work, turned her locker upside down, and even tried to damage her protective gear. Brenda was surprised by how angry these men were, and she often felt like giving up. But she knew it was important to keep going. In school, Brenda had studied the women's suffrage (voting rights) movement from the 1800s, and thinking of the people who led that struggle gave her the strength to push on.

Brenda spent twenty-four years as a firefighter, eventually becoming a captain. She's proud of the way she opened doors for others: "I think too often young people believe that one person is not enough to make a change. I'm here to tell you that that's not true. It might not be the easiest thing to do, but one person *can* make a change."

* * * * *

▷ THE SUFFRAGE MOVEMENT

In the mid-1800s, many women who had been active in the movement to abolish slavery joined forces to push for suffrage (voting rights) for women. These suffragists were divided about issues such as whether to fight for the voting rights of African American men first and then for women's suffrage and about whether to fight on state-by-state or national levels. There was racial prejudice in the suffrage movement, just as there was in society overall. Black women suffragists were often excluded from white women's organizations and agendas. After a nearly seventy-five-year battle, the Nineteenth Amendment granting women the right to vote finally became law in 1920. The voting rights of African American men and women, however, were constantly challenged and denied. The Civil Rights Act of 1964 was enacted to help make suffrage real for them and for all US citizens.

Title VII of the Civil Rights Act

In 1964, a federal law was passed called Title VII of the Civil Rights Act, which made it illegal for employers to discriminate against employees on the basis of sex, race, color, national origin, or religion. However, passing a law doesn't always mean that attitudes change, as Brenda Berkman found out. Discrimination still happens, and sometimes people are afraid to speak up. But they don't have to do it alone: there are lots of organizations to help them fight for their legal rights.

Brenda Berkman proved that women could make it as firefighters, and in 1983, Sally Ride did the same for astronauts, becoming the first American woman in space. Ten years after Ride's momentous trip, **Mae Jemison** pushed the barrier even further as the first African American woman to travel in space, on NASA's *Endeavour* shuttle.

Growing up on the South Side of Chicago, Mae felt she was similar to other kids—she liked stars, dinosaurs, dancing, and space. Her parents made her feel she could do anything, and Mae never doubted what the future held: "Growing up, I fully expected to go into space."

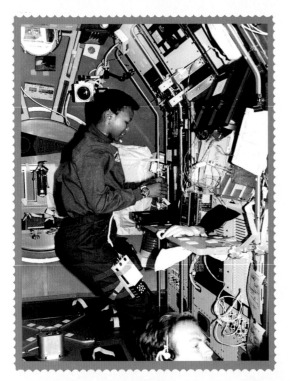

Mae was partly inspired by one of her favorite TV shows, the science fiction series *Star Trek*. Set in the twenty-third century on a vessel that explored new planets, *Star Trek* "had people from all around the world on the bridge of the ship—it even had an alien!" remembers Mae. One of the characters was communications officer Lieutenant Uhura, played by African American actress Nichelle Nichols; seeing a woman of color doing a technical job in space helped Mae believe she could achieve that, too. In fact, NASA asked Nichelle to use her popularity to help them recruit minority and female personnel.

"Growing up, I fully expected to go into space."

Mae studied biomedical engineering in medical school but didn't plan on being a doctor for her whole career—she saw it as

MERCURY 13

The story of women in the US space program started in 1960, when women were invited to pass the same tests that NASA was putting the men through. Twenty women were in the trial, and thirteen passed; they became known as the Mercury 13. In some ways, women were even better astronaut candidates than men because they were usually smaller and weighed less, which meant that they would need less oxygen and other resources on board the shuttle. But since only military test pilots were allowed to become astronauts, and women couldn't be military test pilots, NASA never planned to send them on missions. Though the Mercury 13 stayed earthbound, they paved the way for others. In the 1990s, Eileen Collins became the first woman pilot astronaut, and in 2007, Peggy Whitson became the first female commander of the International Space Station. As of 2016, sixty women from around the world have flown in space.

a stepping-stone to her future in science. Once she became an astronaut with NASA, Mae understood the impact and meaning of what she was doing. "The fact that I was the first woman of color to go into space meant that I had a responsibility to use my perspective and my background to bring a different set of possibilities to the equation. . . . The perspective that stuck with me is that I am as much a part of this universe as any speck of stardust. That perspective of belonging was what was important to me."

> **"The fact that I was the first woman of color to go into space meant that I had a responsibility to use my perspective and my background to bring a different set of possibilities to the equation. . . ."**

Katherine Johnson

Katherine Johnson, a brilliant African American mathematician, made her mark on the history of space travel without ever leaving the ground. She worked for NASA in 1953 doing math calculations as a "human computer." She faced racial and gender barriers but persisted, reminding people that she'd done the work and belonged in the important meetings. Her complex calculations helped NASA with the first successful space flights. Once computers replaced humans, astronaut John Glenn asked Katherine to personally check the math needed to get him home after orbiting the earth. In 2015, President Barack Obama awarded Katherine the Presidential Medal of Freedom. Her amazing story, along with those of other African American women at NASA, is told in the book and movie *Hidden Figures*.

Robyn Beavers

As a kid, Robyn Beavers was nerdy. She liked math and science but thought that if she pursued those subjects, she'd have to give up "being a girl." One night, she heard astronaut Mae Jemison give a speech on the radio, urging girls to pursue careers in science, and Robyn got inspired: her passion didn't have to be just a dream. In college, she got a degree in civil engineering, which meant it was her job to figure out how to build things. Eventually, she became a "clean energy" expert and helped put ten thousand solar panels on top of Google's headquarters to power our internet searches. Robyn then started designing methods to use wind and water as energy. Robyn continues to think big: "Once you start thinking about the way the world works today, it becomes pretty clear that it could be designed better."

★ ★ ★ ★ ★

Today, thanks to these groundbreakers and others like them, women are working in all types of fields, from entertainment to politics to science, technology, and more. Still, you might find yourself as one of the only girls in a sport or activity you love. If that causes problems for you, or something about it feels extra hard or unfair, think of the women in this chapter. Take a cue from Sheryl Sandberg, Facebook's chief operating officer, who says: **"I was raised to think that I could achieve anything I wanted to achieve."** Let their strength and determination help you power through challenges, and have faith in yourself!

When "NO" Isn't an Option!

Marin Alsop 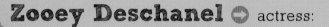 first woman conductor of a major American orchestra:

"When I told my violin teacher [that I wanted to be a conductor], she told me, 'Girls don't do that.' I was devastated. But my mother said, 'You can do anything you want to do, and you can be anything you want to be.'"

Zooey Deschanel actress:

"There have been so many things that people have told me I can't do in my life that I've done, and it feels really nice! Only you know what you can do and can't do."

Val Demings congresswoman and first female chief of police of the Orlando, Florida, police department:

"The more people told me I could not do something, it just made me more and more determined to do just that."

Geraldine Ferraro former congresswoman and vice presidential nominee:

"I think my campaign made a difference. We pulled down the sign from the door of the White House that says, 'Males Only.' If you can take that sign down from the door of the White House with a candidacy, is there any job in this country—or in the world—where any woman would be told, 'Sorry, we're not hiring any women this year'? Or any job where she would be told, 'Sorry, you can't make it'?"

2

BEING THE FIRST

QUICK: THINK OF A time in your life when being first to do something (like play a sport or have a specific task) was exciting and awesome.

Now think of a time when it was totally the opposite, and going first felt scary and lonely.

It can definitely go one way or the other, especially if what you're doing comes with responsibility. Maybe you were the first girl to be head of your student council or a new organization at your school, and you felt like you had to be amazing at it so other girls could take the same position later on.

Sometimes, that pressure is a good thing: many women take on leadership positions because they know their work will inspire others. When **Ruth Simmons** was asked to be the president of Brown University in 2000—making her the first African American president of an Ivy League university—she wanted the job, for sure, but mostly she said yes as she recognized it was too important an opportunity to pass up.

In this chapter you'll also meet women like **Julie Chu**, an Olympic ice hockey player; **Maria Pepe**, who fought for girls to be able to play on Little League team; and **Linda Alvarado**, who created her own construction company. Read on to see what happened when they saw an opportunity to be the first at something that mattered to them, and went for it.

★ ★ ★ ★ ★

Top: Senate women with pay equity activist Lilly Ledbetter; center: Danica Patrick; bottom: Julie Chu.

FIRSTS IN THEIR FIELDS

1967 Muriel Siebert: first woman to own a seat on the New York Stock Exchange (NYSE)

1968 Kathy Kusner: first female licensed horse racing jockey

1976 Barbara Walters: first woman to anchor the nightly news

1981 Jenette Kahn: first female comic book executive

1997 Violet Palmer: first female NBA referee

2007 Marin Alsop: first woman conductor of a major American orchestra

2007 Val Demings: first female police chief of a major city, Orlando, Florida

2011 Kelly Clark: first female snowboarder to successfully complete a 1080 in the women's halfpipe competition

Ruth Simmons was born in Grapeland, Texas, a tiny town across the state from where Sandra Day O'Connor was raised. Since Ruth is African American and grew up during segregation (when black people were not allowed in many schools, restaurants, and other public places) in the 1940s and 1950s, and Sandra is white, their experiences were very different.

Ruth's family had unique challenges in the face of racism, and personal safety was a huge concern for Ruth and her eleven siblings. "We were taught how to walk on a sidewalk and step off the sidewalk when a white person was approaching," Ruth explains. "We were taught never to speak out of turn or to speak in an arrogant or aggressive way. We were taught not to go to certain places."

Ruth's parents were sharecroppers (farmers who pay rent for their land with crops), and she spent her early years on a farm. When she was seven years old, her family moved to Houston. That's when Ruth, like many other women in this book—and maybe even you, too—fell in love with reading.

Ruth was a great student, and in high school she dreamed of continuing her education. "I remember when I asked my mother if I could perhaps go to college one day," Ruth says. "I think the look on her face really said it all: what an impossible idea." Ruth's family supported her but couldn't imagine that college was an option for someone with their background.

Have you thought about going to college? Does your family expect you to go? If not, are there adults in your community who can help you? That's what happened to Ruth. A teacher helped her get a scholarship to Dillard. Her teachers even took clothes out of their own closets for Ruth to take with her to school! And Ruth didn't just get a college degree— she also earned a PhD and many fellowships (programs where you study something specific, usually after graduate school). She eventually became an academic dean and then the president of several universities, including Smith College, Brown University, and Prairie View A&M University, a historically all-black college.

Even in a career full of successes, Ruth experienced unfairness. When she was a vice provost at Princeton University, she learned that a male coworker who had less experience, education, and responsibility was being paid much more than she was. Seems wrong, doesn't it? It is! It's also illegal, but unfortunately it still happens even today. "Most people

Lilly Ledbetter

Like Ruth Simmons, Lilly Ledbetter grew up poor and with limited expectations of what she could achieve. She was raised in Alabama in a house with no running water, electricity, or indoor plumbing and had to walk five miles to catch a bus to school. As she got older, Lilly worked her way up to being a manager at Goodyear Tire and Rubber Company. But she found out she was being paid less than her male coworkers—40 percent less in some instances, even though she had more experience and did a great job. "When I saw how much those men were making, I was devastated and humiliated," remembers Lilly. For more than ten years, she fought for equal pay. In January 2009, President Obama's first act as president was to sign the **Lilly Ledbetter Fair Pay Restoration Act,** which helps make sure that women have equal pay. Lilly's success, like Ruth's, showed that equal pay is always worth fighting for.

never see these differences because of course salaries are hidden, perks are hidden . . . but one day it's disclosed and you discover, my goodness, you've been mistreated for all these years," says Ruth. Once she learned what was going on, she was able to fight against it.

Ruth's dedication to learning and hard work brought her from a sharecropper's farm to some amazing "firsts." She says: "This world I lived in, this world of segregation and bigotry, wasn't really the real world. I knew that. What I had to do was go outside it. And that's what everybody has to do: they have to find a way to be a part of that larger world."

★ ★ ★ ★ ★

> **"Team sports are great for the growth of girls and women. . . . We develop so many great characteristics and values."**

When **Julie Chu** was eight years old, growing up in Fairfield, Connecticut, she'd hang out at the ice rink and watch her older brother play ice hockey. One day, she noticed a poster on the wall that said, "Girls Can Play Hockey Too!" and thought, "Maybe this is something *I* can do." Her parents set her up with secondhand gear to see if she'd like it.

She did, and started playing on a boys' team. "I didn't realize how strange that was for some people at the time," Julie remembers. "You could go through an entire season and only see one other girl." At age ten, Julie played in a tournament on a women's team with eighteen-year-olds and realized, "Hey, I might actually be pretty good at this game."

> **"Hey, I might actually be pretty good at this game."**

Still, she wasn't sure if there was a future in it—until 1998, when women's ice hockey officially became an Olympic sport. The US women took home gold medals that year, and Julie dreamed of one day putting on her own USA hockey jersey. It didn't take long: she made the 2002 Olympics. She was nineteen years old and the first Asian American woman to play for the US Women's team.

"I was playing against older women that were more experienced, stronger, faster, everything!" Julie remembers. "And yet, they did everything they could to help bring me along."

During her career, Julie competed in four Winter Olympics, winning a medal each time, making her one of the most decorated Winter Olympians. Now it's Julie's turn to bring along new generations of players, coaching college hockey and mentoring young girls on the rink. "Team sports are great for the growth of girls and women," she says. "We develop so many great characteristics and values."

* * * * *

Danica Patrick

The first time Danica Patrick drove a go-kart, she crashed into a building. That didn't stop the ten-year-old from falling in love with "open-wheel" racing. When she was sixteen, Danica was offered an amazing opportunity to train and race in the British National Series and spent three years living in England. After she came back to the US, Danica became only the fourth woman ever to compete in the legendary Indy 500. She continued to climb in the IndyCar standings but kept missing out on that first-place finish. Finally, in 2008, she made her mark **as the first-ever female winner of the Indy Japan 300.** "My parents never let me or my sister think that we couldn't do something," Danica says. "We had Barbie dolls. But then we also had four-wheelers." Her advice to anyone hoping to be a race car driver? "Don't be like me, be better than me!"

➡ A KID'S TAKE

"It's fascinating how Danica Patrick is a woman in a male-dominated industry but has made history by being the first woman ever to win an IndyCar race. What's amazing about that is that even though she had a few setbacks, she never stopped trying."

—Kendall, age 12

By the time Julie Chu was born in 1982, few sports were off-limits to girls. But things were quite different when **Maria Pepe** tried to play Little League in the spring of 1972.

When she was a young girl, Maria had some killer baseball skills and was invited to try out for a Little League team called the Hoboken Young Democrats. "I made it to the second tryout, and then I was put onto the team," Maria recalls. She was super excited—she loved baseball and wearing a uniform. When people asked her what she wanted to be when she grew up, Maria always said: "A Yankee."

Maria was the starting pitcher, and soon people began noticing that she was a girl—and they didn't like it. The Little League rule book said girls weren't allowed to play. At first, her coach stood up for Maria; but after the second or third game, he offered her the job of being scorekeeper, fearing that the town's league was in jeopardy. Maria wasn't happy about that. "I could not just sit there and take score, because I wanted to be out there," she says.

Maria remembers wishing she were a boy so she could be on the field and not on the sidelines. "I used to have these conversations with God," says Maria, who was raised Catholic. "Why did you give me this ability?" she would wonder.

News about Maria being removed from the game caught the headlines of local New Jersey newspapers. Maria's family got a call from the National Organization for Women (see chapter 7), and after he hung up, Maria's father explained, "They feel bad about what happened to you playing ball, and they would like to file a complaint with the New Jersey

▶ YOUNG & BOLD: SAM GORDON

When Sam Gordon was nine years old, she had a record football season: she scored twenty-five touchdowns and ran more than two thousand yards! Since then, her YouTube videos of playing football have been seen by millions of people and even landed her face on a Wheaties cereal box and in a 2019 Superbowl ad. In 2015, Sam started a girls' football league, with three hundred other girls participating. Sam loves the fact that she's inspired lots of other girls to think of football as something they can play, too.

Division on Civil Rights on your behalf. I feel that they should go ahead and do that."

Maria's legal case lasted two years. "They had physiologists testifying whether girls were mentally equipped to play ball with boys," says Maria. "They had doctors testifying about the strength of girls' bones compared to boys'." Hard to imagine, right? In the end, judge Sylvia Pressler ruled in Maria's favor. Her ruling stated that Little League is as American as the hot dog and apple pie, and there's absolutely no reason why girls should be shut out of that part of American life.

Maria will never forget the day she heard the ruling. Her father told her, "You know, Maria, they ruled in your favor." By that time, Maria was too old to play, but her father reminded her that she'd opened the doors for all the girls who would come after her. Maria says, "That's my gift, is that I get to see so many girls actually enjoying it and participating in it and not being discriminated against . . . but actually being encouraged to grow in the sport."

> **"That's my gift. . . . I get to see so many girls actually enjoying it . . . and not being discriminated against. . . ."**

* * * * *

Linda Alvarado always had a passion for construction, so it's no wonder she became the first woman and Latina to own a construction company. She was also the first Latina owner of a major league baseball team: the Colorado Rockies.

To make ends meet during college, Linda applied to work with the groundskeeping staff on her campus but was turned away because she was a girl. "Do you not understand girls do food service, boys do groundskeeping?" the manager told her, and sent her off to meet with her college advisor for counseling.

Eventually, Linda convinced the manager to let her join his staff, and she loved the work. Many of her coworkers weren't used to seeing women in that role.

To get her first job in construction, Linda used only her initials on the application so people wouldn't know she was a woman—a habit she continued in her career. When people saw "Linda," they assumed a secretary had filled out the form. *Better to surprise them*, Linda thought.

Linda first started a small business that repaired curbs, gutters, and sidewalks. After she was rejected by five banks for a loan to expand her company, her parents—who didn't have a lot of money—mortgaged their home to get a $2,500 loan for their daughter. From there, Linda grew Alvarado Construction bigger and bigger, and people took notice. Eventually, as a general contractor, she built impressive projects like the Denver Broncos' Mile High Stadium and Denver Botanic Gardens.

Linda has a great philosophy that's worked for her: "Don't find excuses. Find reasons to succeed."

★　★　★　★　★

For the women in this chapter, doing something they loved, something they were *awesome* at, also meant they were breaking new ground for future generations. "I didn't want to be a girl who happened to be their teammate," Julie Chu says. "I wanted to play well and earn the ice time I had."

➡ WHAT IS AFFIRMATIVE ACTION?

Affirmative Action is a policy that aims to help people who are likely to suffer from discrimination due to factors such as their race or gender; it helps them be fairly considered when it comes to getting hired for a job or admitted to a school. In the US, many people believe Affirmative Action is important because it helps make sure the American workforce reflects our country's diversity. Other people have challenged these policies, saying that less qualified candidates are hired or promoted before other, more qualified candidates. Linda Alvarado gives thanks to affirmative action: **"It was not a guarantee for success, but it was a window that could be opened for that opportunity. And what women were looking for was not that guarantee that they would succeed, but at least the opportunity to try."**

The Equal Employment Opportunity Commission

The Equal Employment Opportunity Commission (EEOC) was created in 1965 to enforce Title VII of the Civil Rights Act (see chapter 1), which was supposed to ban unequal treatment on the basis of race, religion, and gender. The EEOC was quickly flooded with reports of discrimination. One of the first complaints came from a group of flight attendants. "They hadn't even unpacked the typewriters," remembers former flight attendant **Dusty Roads,** when she, Jean Montague, and others arrived at the EEOC headquarters in Washington, DC. Their complaint: the airlines were forcing women to retire at the age of thirty-two. "Their assumption was that by thirty-two, you should be at home, married, and having children," Montague says. After years of fighting, the airlines were found guilty of gender discrimination. By 2017, the EEOC received an average of forty-five thousand complaints each month.

Other women have similar sentiments. "It's wonderful to be the first to do something," says Sandra Day O'Connor, "but if I did not do the job well enough, there might not be a second woman on the court." Ruth Bader Ginsburg feels the same way: "If you were called on and didn't perform well, you felt you would be failing not only yourself but all women."

What about you? Does the thought of being the first girl to do something in your school or community excite you or scare you? Does it make you shy away from activities or interests, or does the idea get you fired up? I hope you'll look for opportunities to challenge the way things are and explore your passions even if few—or no—other girls are doing it.

Judaline Cassidy

As a young girl in Trinidad and Tobago, Judaline Cassidy was shy and had little confidence. Her great-grandmother encouraged her by telling her she could be anything she wanted to be. Judaline couldn't afford university, but because her country offered a free education in the trades, she trained to be a plumber and fell in love with it. **"I get to create things with my hands, and I get to solve a puzzle,"** Judaline says. When she moved to New York City and tried to join the local plumbers union, she was told to "go home and do the dishes." She felt crushed but stayed focused on doing her best work. Eventually a male colleague stood up for her, insisting she be let into the union as its first woman member. Later, after six or seven attempts, she was elected union leader—once again, the first woman in Staten Island local union 371 to do so. Judaline also launched Tools & Tiaras, an organization that inspires and teaches girls the skills to work as electricians, carpenters, plumbers, and auto mechanics.

FAMILY MATTERS

IS THERE SOMEONE IN your family who inspires you? Your mom, your dad, a grandparent, an aunt, or even a sibling? Maybe you want to be just like her or him when you're older . . . or maybe this person inspires you by showing you what you *don't* want (which can also be really helpful). Maybe you're growing up without a mom or female role model, and that's a big part of who you are.

In this chapter, you'll meet some women whose families greatly influenced them in one way or another. Author **Judy Blume** worried that her mother regretted not pursuing her dream of being a teacher, and Judy was deliberate about not repeating the same pattern. It helped that she was starting her profession just as the women's movement of the 1970s was gaining visibility. **Sandra Cisneros**, author of *The House on Mango Street*, felt that her father was her biggest cheerleader. **Temple Grandin**, professor of animal science and author, credits her mother for helping her learn how to navigate life with autism. **Shelly Lazarus**, an advertising executive, was on track to become a wife and mom, just like her mother, but eventually headed up a big advertising firm. **Ursula Burns** became top boss at Xerox, something her mother could never have dreamed of.

It's very likely that your family is influencing you in big and small ways. And it's just as likely that you're influencing others in more ways than you can imagine!

★ ★ ★ ★ ★

Top: Barack and Michelle Obama; center, left: Judy Blume; center, right: Lena Dunham; bottom, left: Sandra Cisneros; bottom, right: Temple Grandin.

Are You There, God? It's Me, Margaret. Tales of a Fourth Grade Nothing. Superfudge. Chances are, you or someone you know has read these or other books by **Judy Blume.** She's one of the most popular children's book authors in history, known for talking honestly about things that kids deal with, like friendship, sibling relationships, puberty, and racism. She started out writing for kids because she felt like one herself. "I was more comfortable with the twelve-year-old me than the thirty-year-old me. I knew who I was when I was twelve."

Judy grew up in suburban New Jersey, got married when she was twenty-one (and still in college), and by the time she was twenty-five, she had two young children. Her husband was a lawyer, and the breadwinner of the family (meaning his salary supported them). Like many other women in the 1950s, Judy thought she was supposed to be happy with her quiet and predictable life: getting married, having babies, and being a full-time mom. Problem was, she wasn't! She loved caring for her two young children, but something was missing. She dreamed of doing something creative and challenging.

Judy made some felt pictures as decorations for children's bedrooms and sold them to Bloomingdales, a department store. But there was another spark inside her: she'd always

▶ ARE YOU THERE, GOD? IT'S ME, MARGARET

Margaret, the main character of this popular novel, is a lot like the book's author. "She's a late developer," Judy says. "She is desperate to be normal, and God is her confidante, as he was mine or she was mine." Like Margaret, Judy was always fascinated by puberty. "I did all those exercises; I pricked my finger and put blood on a sanitary napkin to see what it would be like. I wore it to school to prove to my friends that I had my period. I lied about getting my period, which I didn't get until I was fourteen." Judy first learned about menstruation from her father when she was about nine years old, which ended up just being confusing to her. He talked about her "lunar cycle." "I thought when the moon is full every woman in the world has this wonderful thing happening to her!" she remembers.

loved books and was bursting with ideas of her own. "I had stories in my head all the time," she remembers. With the $350 she earned from the felt pictures, she bought an electric typewriter and started putting those stories onto paper. She typed up rhyming picture books, illustrated them herself, and sent them to publishers, who said *no* over and over again. "With each rejection, it was tough," Judy remembers. "But each time, I got a little stronger."

> **"With each rejection, it was tough," Judy remembers. "But each time, I got a little stronger."**

Judy sharpened her skills and connected with other aspiring authors while taking a course on writing for young people. After she sold a couple of short stories, she sent off a book manuscript to a new publishing company. Days later, her phone rang with the offer to publish her first book.

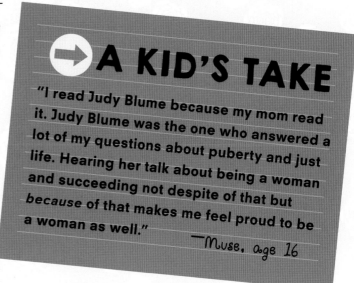

A KID'S TAKE

"I read Judy Blume because my mom read it. Judy Blume was the one who answered a lot of my questions about puberty and just life. Hearing her talk about being a woman and succeeding not despite of that but because of that makes me feel proud to be a woman as well."
— Muse, age 16

More than fifty years later, Judy's written twenty-nine books that have been translated into thirty-two languages, and won many awards. These books have helped many young readers over the years, but Judy says her writing has helped her, too. "It allowed me to soar emotionally and intellectually," she says. Even though she took a different path in life than her parents did, Judy adds, "My mother was my biggest fan."

> **"My mother was my biggest fan."**

When it comes to imagining your future self, Judy has some advice for you: "Don't let anybody discourage you. If you feel it, deep inside, if you need to do it, then you have to go out there even though there will always be people who tell you you can't, you're not good enough."

★ ★ ★ ★ ★

Sandra Cisneros, also a well-known author, says her mother nurtured her into the woman she is. Sandra's mom had worked in a factory and gave up her job once she had seven kids at home. "I remember as a child she would tell me: 'You better learn how to type so that you can be a secretary, because their hands are clean and they wear nice clothes,'" Sandra says. Sandra was disappointed that her mother had such limited hopes for her, but she also understood that was the reality when her mother was Sandra's age.

Sandra's family, culture, and community surrounded her with creativity. "I had a childhood that was filled with things of the spirit, and I think many artists have that kind of childhood," she says. As she climbed trees, she would talk to them, and in her imagination, they would talk back. "I think art is there to heal us, to transform pain into enlightenment. I feel very lucky that my work goes out and that I witness that transformation."

> **"I had a childhood that was filled with things of the spirit. . . ."**

The House on Mango Street is one of Sandra's best-known books. It's about a young girl, Esperanza, who grows up in a poor Latino Chicago neighborhood—a barrio. She looks for a better life and promises to come back for those she left behind. Sandra grew up in a similar neighborhood. "I felt trapped and frightened in the barrio," she explains. Since its publication in 1984, *The House on Mango Street* has been translated into twenty languages and has sold over six million copies.

Sandra was also a daddy's girl. "My theory is that women who have fathers who adore them—it builds a core of self-esteem. Even though life will give you the beatings that every woman has, if you have that sense of love and sense of well-being, I think that's so essential." Sandra has many friends who share a common bond of being their father's favorite. "Our fathers believed in us, and somehow that allows you to have, like, a little life jacket to survive all of the deluges that life is going to give you."

> **"My theory is that women who have fathers who adore them— it builds a core of self-esteem."**

* * * * *

Family can be influential in many ways, like helping you come up with a business idea! **Jennifer Hyman** was visiting family over Thanksgiving one year when she noticed that her sister had a super-expensive dress she'd worn only once. What a waste! This got Jennifer thinking: What if we could rent fancy clothes instead of buying them? She then co-founded Rent the Runway, a company with shops and a website where you can do just that. "I am so optimistic for the future of women in business," Jennifer says.

Temple Grandin has become an expert on animal behavior—there was even a movie made about her, starring Claire Danes. But she couldn't have gotten to where she is today without her mother's help.

Temple is autistic, a condition with which one in eighty-eight US children has been diagnosed. For Temple, it has meant that she is a visual thinker—she sees words as a series of pictures (autism can mean different things for different people). "I like the logical way I think, and I wouldn't want to change that," Temple says. Temple didn't speak until she was four years old. "My mother was very crucial for my success," she says. "Autistic kids sometimes don't want to try something new. [My mother] had a really good idea of how to stretch me. One of the things she did was had me dress up in my Sunday best and greet her dinner party guests and then serve them hors d'oeuvres. So I learned how to shake hands, because you've got to teach social skills to little kids with autism."

Temple's mother continued to guide Temple throughout her childhood. When Temple was fifteen years old, she started having terrible panic attacks. All she wanted to do was become a recluse in her room, but her mother wouldn't allow it. She had Temple spend time at her aunt's ranch. Turns out that Temple loved being on the ranch, and that's where her passion for studying animals began.

> "I like the logical way I think, and I wouldn't want to change that."

Temple now consults with the meat industry to develop more humane innovations in the slaughter of cattle. "We've got to give that animal a life that's worth living for the time that it is here," she says.

* * * * *

Advice from Family

Tina Tchen ➡ former assistant to President Obama and chief of staff to former first lady Michelle Obama:

> "One of the things I did learn from my parents was 'You should be involved in your community. You should care about what's going on around you, in the world, and if you see something that troubles you, you should get involved in it!'"

Lena Dunham ➡ writer, director, actor, producer:

> "My father's a big source of advice, and he always said, 'You should go where there's a "you-shaped" hole in the world, where you see a space for yourself to make a difference and be satisfied.'"

Tamika Catchings ➡ Women's National Basketball Association (WNBA) champion:

> "My parents were like, 'You know what? If anybody can [become a professional athlete], you can.'"

Elaine Chao ➡ US secretary of transportation:

"**I believe that my upbringing made me more compassionate, more empathetic, and a better leader—and that I attribute to my parents. They always encouraged us to expand our world. They so believed that their daughters could achieve great things in this great country called America.**"

Ruth Simmons ➡ PhD, university president:

"**[My mother told me,] 'Never consider yourself better than any other human being.'**"

Michelle Obama ➡ former first lady:

"**My brother and I were blessed with something far more valuable [than money], because our parents truly gave us unconditional love and encouragement to go places they never imagined for themselves.**"

Anna Maria Chávez ➡ former chief executive officer (CEO), Girl Scouts of the USA:

"**I was very fortunate because, growing up, I had two very strong mentors, and they happened to be women. They were my grandmother and my mother. They really wanted me to learn about business, community service, and being an activist at the local level.**"

In 1968, advertising executive **Shelly Lazarus** enrolled in business school four days after she graduated from college. "I went from an all-women's college to a class of three hundred where there were four women," says Shelly. She pursued an MBA degree (master of business administration) so she could get a job to support her and her husband while he finished medical school. "I never had aspirations, but on the other hand, I never had a sense that a woman couldn't do anything," says Shelly.

At business school, Shelly discovered marketing and fell in love with it. She soon had an internship at General Foods, a company that sold packaged food, and her internship turned into a full-time job. When two of her male colleagues left to fight in the Vietnam War, she took on their workload. "I did the work of two experienced men," Shelly remembers. "I had no idea what I was doing, but I just loved it." Shelly then took a job at the advertising firm Ogilvy & Mather and eventually became the CEO of the company. A CEO, which stands for "chief executive officer," is in charge of a business the way a principal is in charge of a school; sometimes the CEO is even the person who founded the company.

Shelly also had children and, like many other women, sometimes found it difficult to balance work and family. In fact, she was at a field day for her son's school when she got the call asking her to be CEO!

At first, being a woman in advertising was an advantage. Many

> **"I had no idea what I was doing, but I just loved it."**

▷ YOUNG & BOLD: McKENNA PETERSON

Twelve-year-old McKenna Peterson was flipping through a Dick's Sporting Goods catalog when she noticed there wasn't a single photo of a girl playing sports. She wrote a letter to Dick's, explaining why it's important for girls to be in their catalog. The CEO responded: "We clearly messed up, and I can personally guarantee that next year's basketball catalog will prominently feature female athletes, as it should have this year." If you see or hear something that doesn't feel right, speaking up really can make a difference!

of the products her company worked on were being marketed to women, but there were few of them at the office to actually weigh in. Shelly's colleagues would often ask her, "Well, Shelly, what do women think?"

Shelly's team at Ogilvy took on clients like American Express and Dove soap. When American Express wanted women customers, Shelly had a simple idea: show women using an American Express card. For Dove, she tried to show a new definition of beauty by celebrating lots of different women's body shapes and sizes—something that hadn't been done before—in their Campaign for Real Beauty. The campaign was motivated by some depressing facts: only 2 percent of women in the world considered themselves "beautiful"! If someone asked you if you considered yourself beautiful, how would you answer? We hope that whatever your definition is, you see and feel it in yourself!

Shelly didn't set out to change the way advertising represents and connects to women. She found something she loved to do and let her passion take her from there. "The great thing about living in this age that we're in," says Shelly, "is that women are allowed to have any ambition that they can dream of. . . . If you can dream it, you can do it."

"If you can dream it, you can do it."

★ ★ ★ ★ ★

When **Ursula Burns** started working at Xerox right after college in the early 1970s, she couldn't have predicted that someday, she'd become head of the company. "I think in the first ten years I didn't even know there was a CEO [chief executive officer]," she says. Which makes it even more amazing that she became the first black female CEO of a Fortune 500 company (a company that makes *Fortune* magazine's annual list of the most financially successful companies). She is one of only a few dozen women ever to be the CEO of a megacorporation. That's a lot of firsts! "When I was told formally that I became a CEO, I couldn't believe it," says Ursula. "The day that it was announced, I remember saying, 'This is the best thing in the world.'"

Born in 1958, Ursula grew up at the height of the civil rights movement. "My mother was a single parent. We were very, very poor," says Ursula. But her mother made sure her kids—Ursula, her brother, and her younger sister—got a good education. She also had a strong sense of community and family, which provided some safety in her neighborhood, where drugs were rampant. "We lived in a bad place, but we were not bad people," remembers Ursula. "Most of the people who we knew were just trying hard to make a better life."

Ursula absolutely did create that better life for herself. Looking back at her career, she realizes she had three big breaks:

1 She had a great first boss. Ursula would design an experiment, and he'd figure out a way to build it.

2 She has a wonderful husband. They were coworkers for years before they dated. Before she met him, she used to rush down a long corridor on her way to lunch, always busy with work. She never stopped to chat with coworkers. A colleague gave her some advice: "Step out. There's other stuff that's happening." Ursula started to talk to her coworkers, and that's how she met the man who became her husband!

3 At her future husband's urging, Ursula attended a Quality of Work Life Council meeting, which addressed diversity issues within the Xerox company. At the meeting, Ursula was offended by one statement about how minority employees might not be as skilled as others. After the meeting, she confronted the person who made the comment. Turns out he was the head of Xerox! Soon Ursula was invited for a meeting in his office, and he became an important friend and mentor.

Ursula's mentor was the exact opposite of her: he was a white middle-class conservative, and a Republican. She was an urban, liberal black woman from New York City. "It was interesting that I could form a friendship with somebody who was so different," says Ursula. "We argued about everything." What she learned was this: "You could actually like and respect somebody who was so different. This was a defining moment not only in work but also personally for me."

The reason Ursula spoke up in that meeting was largely due to her mother's advice. She says, "I learned from my mother that if you have a chance to speak, you should speak. If you have an opinion, you should make it be known."

> **"I learned from my mother that if you have a chance to speak, you should speak. If you have an opinion, you should make it be known."**

* * * * *

Family can inspire us, but sometimes our lives are changed by a teacher, a coach, someone in our community . . . or even a fictional character. Take it from Ruth Simmons and Mae Jemison: Ruth didn't think a college education would be possible for her until a high school teacher convinced her to apply and helped get her a scholarship, and Mae was inspired by a TV character to go into space.

We also don't have to have our dreams and goals all figured out right away, as Ursula's and Shelly's stories remind us. If you pursue things you enjoy, stay true to who you are, and keep yourself open to new possibilities, there's no limit to where you'll go.

Other Female CEOs

SARA BLAKELY

had the idea for Spanx, "slimming" undergarments, and at forty-one became the youngest self-made female billionaire. She spent two years developing the invention, writing her own patent, and calling hosiery manufacturers before launching her products.

ANDREA JUNG

graduated from Princeton University in 1979. Twenty years later, she became the CEO of Avon Worldwide, becoming chairwoman in 2001.

SHEILA LIRIO MARCELO

emigrated to the US from the Philippines when she was six years old. She wanted to be an entrepreneur *and* make a difference in people's lives. She founded and became the CEO of Care.com, a website that helps match families all over the world with professional caregivers.

4

RETHINKING FAILURE

HERE'S A SIMPLE TRUTH: we all make mistakes. Messed up on a school test? Check. Didn't play your best in a game? Been there. The truth is, what matters most when it comes to mistakes is how we react to them.

It's easy to get obsessed with the idea of doing everything perfectly. But what if failure wasn't something to be afraid of? What if, instead, it was a chance to learn, grow, and find better ways to reach your goals?

For fashion designer **Diane von Furstenberg**, a drop in sales motivated her to work harder, dream bigger, and achieve even more success. Musician **Alicia Keys** took on too much responsibility too quickly and had to refocus on what was most important to her. Neither **Hillary Clinton** nor **Mazie Hirono**, a US senator from Hawaii, gave up after losing an election. And tennis superstar **Serena Williams** never let a setback get her down for long.

The women in this chapter have had some epic fails but have emerged from them stronger than before. They might just inspire you to look at your next "disaster" in a whole new light.

★ ★ ★ ★ ★

Diane von Furstenberg is one of the biggest names in fashion. Referred to as DVF, she's known for creating a certain style of wrap dress that she made popular in the 1970s. "I

Top: Serena Williams; center, left: Alicia Keys; center, right: Geraldine Ferraro; bottom: Hillary Clinton.

Feel like a woman, Wear a dress!

never knew what I wanted to do, but I knew the kind of woman I wanted to be," Diane says. "I wanted to be an independent woman, a woman who could pay for her bills, a woman who can run her own life—and I became that woman."

> **"I wanted to be an independent woman, a woman who could pay for her bills, a woman who can run her own life—and I became that woman."**

Diane was born in Belgium in the 1940s. Her mother had survived the Holocaust, during which millions of Jews and other Europeans were killed by Nazis. She taught Diane that "fear is not an option." When Diane was twenty-three, she married a German prince—but she wanted a career, not just a life of being a princess. She worked for a textile manufacturer in Italy, which made fabric, and the factory also had a printing press. This gave Diane an idea: use them both and make a simple silk jersey dress. Before moving to the US with her husband, Diane convinced her boss to let her take a few dress samples with her and try to sell them in America. She didn't realize it at the time, but that was the first step toward what would become her iconic wrap dress.

One of Diane's first moves was to take out a small ad in *Women's Wear Daily*, a popular fashion magazine. "I asked a friend of mine to take a picture of me in a dress, and I was sitting on a white cube," Diane explains. When she saw the final picture, she thought the cube was too big and too white, so to fill in the space, she wrote something on the cube that just popped into her head: "Feel like a woman, wear a dress!" That photo and catchphrase became her trademark.

In 1976, Diane was on the cover of *Newsweek* and *Interview* magazines. At just twenty-nine years old, she was totally changing the way women dressed and thought about themselves. "My clothes were very soft and all of a sudden revealed the body," Diane explains.

"It was very much part of a movement of being a woman and enjoying being a woman. I was always a little bit of a feminist. It doesn't mean that if you're a feminist you have to look like a truck driver." After several years of success, Diane learned that what goes up . . . must eventually come down. Her business had grown fast, but sales had slowed and left her with millions of dollars in clothing nobody was buying. In 1983, Diane sold her company.

But her dresses proved timeless. When Diane saw that young women were snapping them up in vintage clothing stores, she created fresh versions of the wrap dress as well as other items, and opened up shops around the world. Today, she's still one of the world's top designers and fashion entrepreneurs; she also helps others by supporting human rights causes and mentoring new designers. "You have to be confident and go for it!" she says.

★　★　★　★　★

Recording artist **Alicia Keys** isn't exactly a name we associate with failure. When she performs songs like "Girl on Fire" and "In Common," people listen. Her powerful, soulful music has sold more than thirty-five million albums and won countless awards. But her journey shows us how sometimes mistakes can actually point us toward the right path.

Alicia was raised by a single mother in New York City who worked hard as a paralegal and passed on her work ethic to Alicia. "She had to be tough on me," Alicia says of her mom. "I was her only daughter, growing up in the city." Alicia found inspiration all over the city, where she saw different kinds of people from all over the world come to chase their dreams.

She started playing piano and singing while she was in elementary school. Mixing talent with hard work paid off: by the time she graduated from the New York Professional Performing Arts School at age sixteen as her class valedictorian, Alicia already had a recording contract with a record label *and* a scholarship to Columbia University. She was set to fly high with her skills as a musician, songwriter, vocalist . . . and producer. Did you know there are producers for music? Every song you hear has a producer working behind the scenes, a lot like a producer on a film, pulling together all the different parts of a song, such as the vocals, the instruments, and the sound mixing, to make it the best it can be.

For Alicia, writing and producing her own music was a no-brainer, but others had trouble accepting it, especially because she was young and a woman. "They just never had a girl like me . . . a tomboy with braids . . . coming in here with these ideas. These different guy producers wrote me off from the beginning. They didn't think I could play, they didn't think I could write, they *definitely* didn't think I could produce. That's the one that bothered me the most."

At the same time, Alicia started college, which turned out to be much more challenging than she thought it would be. She couldn't balance her new career with school, so she dropped out after only four weeks. Soon she also realized that she and her record label weren't a good fit, and she had to get out of her contract. Ouch!

Turns out, that double hit led to something unexpected but beneficial: Alicia started working with a famous record producer who totally "got" her and how she needed to be in charge of her own sound. The result was Alicia's first album, *Songs in A Minor*, which went on to win five Grammy Awards.

Today, Alicia Keys is not only a top recording artist but an activist for causes that impact young people all over the world, such as Keep a Child Alive, which provides medicine to families with HIV and AIDS in Africa. She's driven by her successes as well as her challenges. Says Alicia, "Very early, I was aware that there was a dark side and a light side. I believe I've been put on this earth to definitely spread light."

"They *definitely* didn't think I could produce. That's the one that bothered me the most."

★ ★ ★ ★ ★

Bethany Hamilton

When thirteen-year-old surfer Bethany Hamilton lost her left arm in a shark attack, she could have given up on the sport. Would you have blamed her if she did? But Bethany lived in Hawaii, and surfing had been a huge part of her life since she was four years old. **"I always felt invincible growing up,"** Bethany remembers. She didn't let the attack, and the fact that she was now differently abled, change that . . . or kill her love of surfing. She was back on her board a month later. Since then, she's participated in countless competitions. Her advice for bouncing back after a game-changing experience like hers? "Look to the future, and keep on smiling!"

Hillary Clinton's path has been unique in history: from first lady, to US senator, to secretary of state, to the first woman to run with a major party for president of the United States. The list of what she wanted to be when she was a kid is almost as long: "I wanted to be an astrophysicist, a doctor, a teacher," she says. Whatever her job title, Hillary considers herself a problem solver above all. When she lost her 2016 bid for the presidency, she used it as an opportunity to urge others to try to achieve what she didn't.

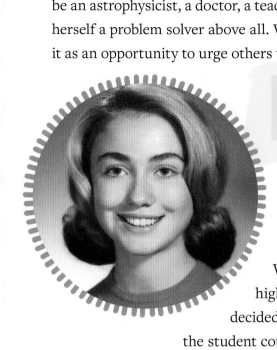

"I wanted to be an astrophysicist, a doctor, a teacher."

Before all that, Hillary started life with a regular childhood: she grew up in a Chicago suburb and attended public schools. Her father was a World War II veteran, and her mother was a stay-at-home mom. When it came time for college, Hillary took the advice of high school teachers who'd gone to women's colleges and decided to go to Wellesley College. There, she became active in the student council. Her father was a conservative Republican, so she joined the College Republicans group. But soon Hillary started thinking, "You know, I'm not sure I really agree with the Republican Party." A professor encouraged her toward an internship in Washington, DC, and the experience helped her figure out that when it came to political views, she was definitely a Democrat.

Hillary was a young adult in the 1960s, when the women's movement was growing. "The women's movement reaffirmed my very fundamental sense of independence and my identity that I was certainly no better but no worse than anybody else, and that I had every right to seek my own identity," she says.

After college, Hillary went to law school, where she excelled and met her future husband. "I fell in love with an extraordinary, complex, dynamic human being," she says. "I had no way of predicting that, yes, I'm going to go to Arkansas and eventually I'm going to marry Bill Clinton. And eventually he's going to become president." She just stayed focused on what was right in front of her.

Hillary made history in 2000 when she became a New York senator—the only first lady ever to be elected to public office. She was reelected in 2006 and then ran for president in 2008. A few days after Barack Obama won that election as the country's first African

American president, Hillary and her husband were on a hike near their home in upstate New York when Obama called to ask for some advice and invite Hillary to a meeting. At that meeting, he asked Hillary to be his secretary of state.

Hillary wasn't so sure about taking the job, but Obama didn't give up. "He batted away the excuses. He agreed with the demands. Eventually I said, 'Okay,'" Hillary recalls.

"I think making the empowerment of women—their political and economic, social empowerment—an integral, essential part of American foreign policy is the right thing to do," says Hillary. "If the nineteenth century was about ending slavery and the twentieth century was about ending totalitarianism, the twenty-first century is ending the pervasive discrimination and degradation of women and fulfilling their full rights."

> **"I think making the empowerment of women—their political and economic, social empowerment—an integral, essential part of American foreign policy is the right thing to do."**

Geraldine Ferraro

In 1984, Geraldine Ferraro was the first woman nominated for vice president by a major political party. It was an epic moment in history. After proudly accepting the nomination at the Democratic National Convention, she said: **"The issue is not what America can do for women, but what women can do for America."** Though she and her running mate, Walter Mondale, lost that election, her nomination inspired many others.

Before the start of her own political career, Wisconsin senator **Tammy Baldwin** remembers watching Ferraro on television. With tears streaming down her face, all Tammy could think was: "My whole future's ahead of me, and I can aspire to anything." Tammy became the country's first openly gay senator.

POLITICAL TRAILBLAZERS

KAY BAILEY HUTCHISON was the first Republican woman to be elected to the Texas House of Representatives. In 1993, she became the first female United States senator from the state of Texas.

GABRIELLE GIFFORDS represented Arizona in the US House of Representatives from 2007 until she retired in 2012. In 2011, Gabby was shot in the head during an assassination attempt and suffered severe brain injuries. Today, she's an activist against gun violence.

ILEANA ROS-LEHTINEN was the first Cuban American and the first Latina to join the US House of Representatives. She was also the first Republican in Congress to support the repeal of the Defense of Marriage Act, which kept same-sex married couples from being recognized as married in all states.

KIRSTEN GILLIBRAND joined the US Senate after Hillary Clinton gave up her seat to become secretary of state. Besides being a great politician, she created an organization called **Off the Sidelines** to help get girls and women involved in politics. "I want women's voices to be heard. If they're being heard in these national debates, we can change the landscape," she says.

★ ★ ★ ★ ★

When senator **Mazie Hirono** was a little girl in Hawaii, running for political office was the furthest thing from her mind. She thought she'd someday grow up to be a therapist or a counselor. But while Mazie was in college in the late 1960s, the Vietnam War was unfolding, and she felt she had to protest against it. "This was the first time I opened my eyes to politics as a way to make social changes," remembers Mazie.

During college, a friend decided to run for state legislature and asked Mazie to be his campaign manager, telling her: "You can't just be protesting and carrying signs. We need to be in a position of making decisions." She joined his team and spent the next ten years running other people's campaigns, while also getting a law degree. Eventually, a politician she knew decided not to run for reelection and suggested Mazie run to take his place. That's a familiar story: many women run for office only after they've been encouraged by others, and Mazie is quick to repay the favor. "I know that encouragement matters to women particularly. I think a diverse Congress makes for better decision making," she says.

In 2002, after many years in public office, Mazie made a run for governor in a historic race: she was the first female Democratic nominee for governor in Hawaii, and her Republican opponent was also a woman. She didn't win, and Mazie says the loss was ". . . a big one. What I learned from that race and that loss was how to win." It was a very public failure, but it helped her figure out that in the future, she needed three components for a winning campaign: resources, a

> **"What I learned from that race and that loss was how to win."**

terrific team of people, and grassroots support (meaning from local people and volunteers). She also learned to focus on issues that are personal for her. For example, Mazie paid her own way through college, so she fights to make sure a higher education is possible for everyone by supporting Pell Grants (grants given by the federal government to students who have financial need) and work-study programs (where you work during college to pay for your tuition).

Mazie's always looking to the future, but she also recognizes her past. "I wouldn't be

Amy McGrath

When Amy McGrath was ten years old, she decided that she wanted to become a naval aviator. But there was a law that prohibited women from flying fighter jets, so Amy wrote letters to lawmakers asking for the law to change. She contacted her congresswoman **Pat Schroeder**, who told her to stick to her dreams and that she was working on changing the law. In 1993, the **Combat Exclusion Policy** was reversed, **enabling women to fight alongside men**. Over her twenty years in the marine corps, Amy McGrath flew eighty-nine combat missions. In 2018, Amy made an unsuccessful bid for Congress. She knew it would be a challenge, but that didn't deter her. "That's what marines do," she says.

sitting here if my mother hadn't made a courageous decision when I was young that she needed to get us away from an abusive husband," Mazie explains. Mazie arrived in Hawaii from Japan when she was eight years old and didn't speak any English. Mazie's mother supported three children by herself despite low-paying jobs, no job security, and no health care benefits. Mazie's greatest fear was that her mother would get sick and there wouldn't be any money. "I just felt so different all the time," she remembers. "I hardly ever talked about my background until I ran for state-wide office in Hawaii."

Now Mazie embraces those struggles and uses what she learned to help the people she represents in Congress. "My mom showed me through her example that one person can make a difference," she says, "because she totally changed my life by bringing me to this country."

YOUNG & BOLD: SOPHIE CRUZ

Sophie Cruz was only seven years old when she gave a powerful speech at the 2017 Women's March in Washington, DC, a massive demonstration in solidarity for women's rights, among many other issues. Sophie was born in the US, which makes her a US citizen, but her parents are undocumented immigrants from Mexico. "We are here together making a chain of love to protect our families," she said. **"Let us fight with love, faith, and courage so that our families will not be destroyed."**

* * * * *

Politicians like Hillary and Mazie have learned from their losses . . . and so have athletes like tennis legend **Serena Williams**.

Serena was born in Michigan, the youngest of five sisters. When she was very little, her father moved their family to Compton, California, a rough neighborhood outside of Los Angeles. (Basketball star Lisa Leslie, featured in chapter 8, is also from Compton.) Serena says, "He wanted to make sure we would be tough enough to handle lots of different situations that we may face in our lives. He also didn't want us to expect an easy life." By the age of three, Serena and her big sister Venus were playing tennis on the public courts of Compton with their father as coach and mentor.

Serena was small for her age, and when she first started playing tournaments, she had no power. "I hit lots of soft balls . . . but I never gave up," says Serena. Serena and Venus came to be known as the Williams sisters. Soon they started winning big tournaments, making professional tennis more diverse. Serena remembers: "I didn't know that we would influence a whole nation and culture and world to start playing."

But it was not all victories and triumphs. Serena would have an incredible winning streak, then lose matches she was expected to win. She battled hard against regular rivals, including her own sister. And in 2010, Serena came up against a huge challenge: a series of health scares that included blood clots in both lungs. She was forced to take a long break from tennis. A year later, Serena was back on the court, and by 2013 she'd reclaimed her title as the number one women's player in the world. "I felt different," she says of how the experience changed her. "I felt like I'd been given a second chance, like if I didn't win, I'll just be alive . . . and I started playing better because I wasn't so uptight . . . I had nothing to lose."

> "I felt like I'd been given a second chance, like if I didn't win, I'll just be alive . . . and I started playing better because I wasn't so uptight . . . I had nothing to lose."

In 2015 *Sports Illustrated* named her Sportsperson of the Year. By 2017, Serena had won a whopping twenty-three Grand Slam Tennis Championships (the Grand Slams are the four most important tournaments in the world), and today she is considered one of the greatest players of all time. In 2018, she gave birth to a daughter, Alexis Olympia, and was back on the courts a few months later. She's accomplished all that she has despite lots of setbacks and unexpected losses . . . or maybe she's made it happen because those things just made her push harder.

* * * * *

After meeting the women in this chapter, you may want to ask yourself:

What happened the last time I failed? Did it ruin my life . . . or did things end up okay?

Did I learn something that was useful?

Is fear of "messing up" keeping me from trying new things or taking chances?

If your answer to any (or most, or all) of these questions is "Yeah!", consider looking at mistakes and setbacks as positives instead of negatives. These moments could be great chances to discover new things about yourself and to move forward in amazing new ways.

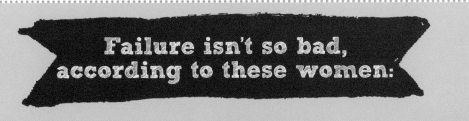

Failure isn't so bad, according to these women:

LISA LESLIE ➡ basketball player: "One of the first moments I faced failure was in the tenth grade. There were four seconds left on the clock, and I missed the layup. It was the state championships. I was on the floor crying. A week later my mom said, 'You can't do everything, Lisa. All you can do is your best.'"

LENA WAITHE ➡ writer and actor: "I don't know if I believe in failures. Everything is a learning moment, and it's something to grow from. I think risks should always be taken."

CHRISTY HAUBEGGER ➡ founder of *Latina* magazine: "I've learned very little from success. I've learned everything from failure."

SARA BLAKELY ➡ founder of Spanx: "My dad used to actually encourage me to fail. We would sit at the dinner table, and he would ask us what we had failed at that week. He was giving me such a gift in life, and that was reframing my thinking of failure."

MARTINA NAVRATILOVA ➡ tennis player: "Women are so risk averse. So you fail, so what? Unless it kills you, literally, then you're probably okay and you can do it again. Better! Next time."

SuCHIN PAK ➡ journalist: "Strength is about people that get knocked down and pick themselves up again and again."

VAL DEMINGS ➡ US Representative and former Orlando chief of police: "Had I not had the courage to put myself out there, and not worry if I failed, I would never have been appointed chief of police. I was the first woman to hold that position in the 132-year history of the Orlando Police Department."

PAYING IT FORWARD

HOW MANY TIMES HAS someone asked you, "What do you want to be when you grow up?"

A ton, right? Maybe you always have a reply, or maybe your answer's always changing, or maybe you have no idea—all of those reactions are totally normal. But here's something fun: turn the question around and ask the adults in your life, "When you were a kid, what did *you* want to be when you grew up? Did you end up doing that?"

Chances are, some people will say they did, but most people will say they did not. That's because life has a way of taking us down some unexpected twists and turns. In this chapter, you'll meet women who are great examples of that: **Kathrine Switzer** liked running, but she had no idea it could be a career—for her or others. Ballerina **Misty Copeland** didn't start dancing until she was a teenager, **Sheryl Sandberg** thought she'd work for a cause instead of a big company, **Christy Haubegger** set out to be a lawyer before she started a magazine, and **Janet Mock** wouldn't have dreamed that she would be a role model to those looking beyond the gender binary. What's interesting about all these women is how their unexpected paths led them to pay it forward for women and girls who came after them.

★　★　★　★　★

"I started the Boston Marathon as a girl," says runner **Kathrine Switzer** of a race that made history. "And I finished the Boston Marathon as a grown woman."

Top: Janet Mock; center: Kathrine Switzer; bottom, left: Trisha Prabhu; bottom, right: Chloe Kim.

Kathrine loved to run, and by the time she was in college in the late 1960s, she was competing in track. She made national headlines when she was recruited to a men's track team and finished a one-mile run in 5:58 minutes. That's a fast time for any runner, male or female!

Kathrine set a new goal for herself: to prove to her track coach, Arnie Briggs, that she could run 26 miles, 385 yards (the length of a marathon). At the time many people assumed that sports were bad for women. Hard to believe, right? People thought that being athletic would make women unfeminine, give them big legs, and make them grow a mustache and hair on their chest. "And your uterus was going to fall out," Kathrine recalls people saying. Arnie was teased by his colleagues for supporting Kathrine: "Hey, Arnie, you're gonna ruin that girl," they would tell him.

"I'm going to finish this race on my hands and my knees if I have to, because nobody believes that I can do this."

Kathrine registered for the 1967 marathon as "K. V. Switzer," and the organizers didn't know she was a woman when they received the entry. She started the race, running alongside her coach and her boyfriend at the time. At the two-mile mark, the race director, Jock Semple, tried to remove Kathrine from the course, grabbing her, trying to rip off her number bib, and yelling, "Get the hell out of my race and give me those numbers!" Kathrine's boyfriend pushed Jock out of the way, while her coach told her, "Run like hell."

"I was so humiliated, so ashamed and scared," Kathrine remembers. But instead of giving up, she got angry and said, "I'm going to finish this race on my hands and my knees if I have to, because nobody believes that I can do this." She finished the Boston Marathon in four hours and twenty minutes. After newspapers published photos of the dramatic incident, Kathrine realized what a big deal this was. "I realized that now this was going to change my life. And it was probably going to change women's sports."

Jock Semple never apologized, but five years later, in 1972, after a lot of lobbying (which is when people work hard to convince people, like politicians or race organizers, of something), women

> "I realized that now this was going to change my life. And it was probably going to change women's sports."

were officially allowed in the Boston Marathon. Jock gave Kathrine a big kiss on the cheek, and they eventually became friends. After that, Kathrine focused on organizing opportunities for women runners and getting them allowed into the Olympic marathon, which happened in 1984. Now running is one of the most popular sports for women in the US. And that old bib number—261—that Jock tried to pull off of Kathrine? It has inspired the 261 Fearless movement of women who are reaching out to help girls and women all over the world discover running—and the courage it can bring them. It seems like there's no limit for what women runners can do!

BOSTON MARATHON STATS

In fifty years, women gained almost two hours on their marathon times, while men gained about six minutes!

1967: Kathrine Switzer, USA, 4:20

1967: David McKenzie, New Zealand, 2:15

2017: Edna Kiplagat, Kenya, won the women's race in 2:21

2017: Geoffrey Kirui, Kenya, won the men's race in 2:09

2017: Kathrine Switzer, finished in 4:44, fifty years after her historic race

▶ YOUNG & BOLD: CHLOE KIM

Here's one perk of being a successful athlete: you inspire others to train hard, do their best, and push your sport even further. When Chloe Kim started competitive snowboarding at age six, one of her heroes was halfpipe and superpipe champion **Kelly Clark.** In 2015, when Chloe was fourteen, she competed against Kelly and beat her, becoming the youngest snowboarder to win gold at the Winter X Games. Three years later, Chloe took home a gold medal from the 2018 Winter Olympics. She still gives props to Kelly for being her idol.

Misty Copeland never set out to be a ballerina. When she was thirteen, a teacher told her she "had something" and looked like a dancer. "Ballet was never on my radar," Misty says. "I enjoyed moving, but that's not something I ever thought of as a career. Ballet found me." Within a month, she started taking her first dance class at a Boys & Girls Club. They practiced on the basketball court, and Misty loved it. "I would be waiting at the door with my dance bag, like, 'Let's go, Mom!'" she remembers.

For the next four years, Misty focused on ballet. She was offered a contract by the American Ballet Theater when she was sixteen, but she turned it down in order to finish high school. Misty joined the company a few years later and says that dancing for them "just felt right." "The first time I stepped on the stage at the Metropolitan Opera, I felt that I had made it," she recalls. Another OMG moment for her was when she performed with the rock star Prince at Madison Square Garden. "That's a huge accomplishment for a classical ballet dancer," Misty says. Misty became one of the only African American soloists ever to perform with the American Ballet Theater in New York City; in 2015, she was promoted to principal dancer.

The older Misty gets, the harder dancing gets. It's physically demanding (she rehearses

African American Women in Ballet

Before Misty, a few other African American dancers joined ballet companies. It wasn't easy, and they faced racial discrimination, but they helped pave the way for Misty. In the 1950s, Raven Wilkinson danced with the Ballet Russes (even though she had to paint her face white) and then the Holland National Ballet. Around the same time, Janet Collins danced with the Metropolitan Opera. In 1990, Lauren Anderson became the first African American principal dancer in the Houston Ballet. In 1996, Aesha Ash became a member of the New York City Ballet, where she worked hard to prove that there's more to ballet than being black or white.

seven hours a day, five days a week), so she has to be in great physical shape *and* make her work look effortless. Pressure much? Misty carries another weight on her shoulders as one of the only African American ballet dancers in a major American company. As a minority, she often feels like she's had to work harder than anyone else. But for her, it's completely worth it. "I really understand the magnitude of young girls watching me," Misty says.

Some of what she hears is heartbreaking. "I get so emotional reading letters from young girls who, even as young as seven years old, are being told that they're too black to be in a ballet school," Misty explains, but that only pushes her more. She discovered her passion thanks to others, and now she's passing it on, showing young dancers someone who looks like them and whom they can relate to. "We all look different," she says, "and that's the growth of where ballet is going."

> **"I get so emotional reading letters from young girls who, even as young as seven years old, are being told that they're too black to be in a ballet school."**

★ ★ ★ ★ ★

Do you think of yourself as a geek? If so, **Sheryl Sandberg** has some advice for you. "I was a really serious geek in high school," she says. "It works out. Study harder!" Sheryl knows what she's talking about: she's been in top positions at Google and Facebook, served on the board of directors of Disney and Starbucks, and rubbed elbows with many world leaders. She's also pretty normal—she's a mom, a sister, an aunt, a friend. But she didn't set out to become an influential businesswoman.

Sheryl was born into a middle-class family in Miami, Florida, the oldest of three siblings. Her dad was an eye doctor, and her mom was a teacher and an active community volunteer. As a kid, Sheryl enjoyed studying, and she and her siblings were raised thinking they could do anything. Her brother and sister both grew up to be doctors like their father.

In her senior year of high school, Sheryl was voted Most Likely to Succeed, but she asked a friend on the yearbook staff

> **"I was a really serious geek in high school. . . . It works out. Study harder!"**

to choose someone else. She thought it would make her look uncool; Sheryl points out how even today, successful men are viewed in a good way, but successful women are often seen as unlikable. Sheryl attended Miami public schools and went to Harvard University, something she had never thought was possible. Her father couldn't resist opening her acceptance letter. It was the first time Sheryl remembers seeing her father cry.

After college, Sheryl worked at the World Bank with her former Harvard professor and mentor Larry Summers. It turned out to be an important experience for her; she learned how the government works, and when the job ended, Sheryl's plan was to help others by working in nonprofits. But then she thought twice. "It seemed like what was actually changing people's lives the most was technology," Sheryl says. "People donate organs. People find their birth mothers. People find friends. People even start movements! I had to get over the fact that these were for-profit companies."

▷ YOUNG & BOLD: TRISHA PRABHU

As Sheryl points out, technology can be a lifesaver. Unfortunately, people can also use it to hurt others. Has anyone ever said mean things to you, about you, or to someone you care about on social media? Whether it's online or in real life, this is called "harassment." (Remember firefighter Brenda Berkman's story from chapter 1? And check out coal miner Barbara Burns's experience in chapter 6. They also dealt with harassment.) Luckily, people like Trisha Prabhu are trying to stop bullying, and specifically cyberbullying, which happens online. When Trisha was only fourteen years old, she created ReThink, an app that detects hurtful messages and asks if you're sure you want to send them. Trisha's research found that 93 percent of the time, **teenagers who are prompted to "ReThink" decide not to post a message that's likely to offend someone.** Since then, she's won many awards, including selection as a 2014 Google Global Science Fair finalist.

Sheryl is also passionate about encouraging girls and women to reach their full potential. She started the organization LeanIn.org, which changes the conversation from what women can't do to what we can do. "Be ambitious," Sheryl says. "Start out with big dreams, big goals!"

★ ★ ★ ★ ★

Christy Haubegger has been a magazine publisher, movie producer, and Hollywood agent. Whatever her title, she's had one goal: to change people's ideas about being a Latinx (Latino or Latina) in America.

Christy was born in Houston, Texas, to a Mexican American mother and was adopted into a family where everyone was tall and blond. Although she looked different from her parents, she loved being adopted because she knew her parents chose her. Still, when she'd tag along to the grocery store to read magazines like *Teen* and *Seventeen* in the checkout line, she says they made her feel "really unattractive and left out." Christy rarely saw women in the media who were brown and "round" like her. Still, her parents told her she could do or be anything. "In some ways, I wonder if they were trying to maybe overcompensate for the world," she says.

In college, Christy worked in the Texas legislature and saw firsthand the tremendous impact a public servant can have. She moved on to law school in California, wanting to help people in the Hispanic community by defending them against unfair laws. After taking classes in business and marketing, she wondered: Why wasn't there a magazine for Hispanic women, like *Essence* magazine was for African American women? As a class project, she wrote a business plan for her idea. It was ambitious, for sure, but she kept telling herself, "You can't be what you can't imagine."

Christy decided to make her dream magazine a reality when she graduated. "If I fail miserably," she thought, "I can be a lawyer." She used a classmate's connection to get a fifteen-minute meeting with Ed Lewis, founder of *Essence*. "To make my case, I said, 'Okay, there are going to be more Hispanic women in this country than African American women in about twenty minutes, and we haven't had a magazine yet.'" Ed took the idea to

"You can't be what you can't imagine."

his board, and they agreed to invest in it. In 1996, Christy launched *Latina*. She took a big risk and put an up-and-coming actress on the cover: future star Jennifer Lopez.

The reaction to the magazine was amazing. Latinx readers felt represented for the first time as they read about a Latina astronaut (Ellen Ochoa) and learned makeup tips for darker skin.

Magazines run on advertising, so Christy approached makeup and car companies but got surprising reactions. "I had people ask me, 'Do you think your readers can afford our product?'" Christy's response was: "You're selling a $5.99 lipstick at Walgreens. I know a lot of poor people. They all have lipstick."

Christy didn't just witness this prejudice; she experienced it herself. After an especially successful meeting, she was walking to her hotel room from the ice machine. She was dressed in a business suit, but when another hotel guest asked her if she would also be delivering ice to *her* room. "I thought of, like, ten really good things to say when I got back in the room," she says. But this experience only made Christy more motivated: "Until that woman sees me and thinks, 'Wow, that looks like an entrepreneur,' or 'I bet that's a lawyer'—until that woman sees me and thinks that, we're not done yet."

Christy points out that there's still a lack of Latinx represented in the media. "We're just over five percent of characters in prime time television," she says, even though Latinx constitute over 17 percent of the US population. But she's proud of her accomplishments with *Latina*: "I wanted to change the complexion of the newsstand. For a lot of people, we were the first magazine to put them on a cover. And now you see women like Jennifer Lopez and Salma Hayek, and you think

Rita Moreno

In 1961, Rita Moreno was the first Latina to win an Academy Award for Best Supporting Actress for her role in *West Side Story*. She has also appeared in the film *The King and I* and the TV series *The Electric Company*. **"I have no objection to playing a Hispanic. I have every objection to playing a stereotype,"** says Rita. Who are some of your favorite Latinx actors, singers, or dancers?

that's not just Latina beauty; that's what American beauty looks like. I love having some small hand in changing the notion of what American beauty looks like."

"I love having some small hand in changing the notion of what American beauty looks like."

* * * * *

When **Janet Mock** was in high school, she met a young transgender woman, Wendi, in her grade. "Transgender" means that one's sense of personal identity and gender don't correspond with their birth sex. Wendi became a great friend to Janet and encouraged Janet to be her true self—a girl, not a boy. "I know who you are; stop pretending," Janet recalls Wendi saying. "In calling me out, she brought me in and offered me a safe space to figure out who I was, and to do that in friendship and sisterhood."

Soon after meeting Wendi, Janet stood in front of her class and introduced herself as Janet for the first time. "I've always known that I was a girl," Janet explains. "I didn't have language to pinpoint why. I grappled with harassment, both for my race and also for my gender."

Janet is now a writer, producer, and director, as well as a transgender rights activist. She studied journalism in college and then worked at *People* magazine. "Listening to people's stories and having the power to then frame those stories and contextualize them really became what I wanted to do in life," she says.

After years of sharing other people's stories, Janet decided to tell her own. In 2011, she opened up in the magazine *Marie Claire* about her story of gender struggle, transition, and self-revelation. She later published a memoir about her experiences. She explains, "I had a story to tell, not only about growing up trans but also growing up as a black child in a world where young people, and poor people, and LGBT people are not given the resources to truly thrive in the world."

"Listening to people's stories and having the power to then frame those stories and contextualize them really became what I wanted to do in life."

ADVICE WORTH SHARING

Ursula Burns ➔ former Xerox Corporation CEO:

"Leave behind more than you take, and it will add up to a good life over time. But if you continually go into places and remove stuff and leave voids, then your life will not be successful. You will not be a good person."

Oprah Winfrey ➔ media mogul and philanthropist:

"When people show you who they are, believe them the first time."

Rita Mae Brown ➔ author and activist:

"Honey, worse things have happened to nicer people."

Billie Jean King ➔ tennis champion and activist:

"Champions adjust, and having pressure is a privilege."

Julie Taymor ➔ theater and film director:

"The bigger the risk, the bigger the payoff."

The people in this chapter are proof that starting off with a plan is important, but keeping yourself open to new possibilities can bring you to some amazing people and places. They've shown us that there's no single or "right" way to become your future self.

When you think of successful people, what pops into your head? Money? Power? A fancy-sounding title? For many, those ingredients are definitely part of the recipe. For others, success is all about how happy they are, or making an impact with something they care about, like helping more women realize their potential—and paving the way for others. Our ideas of success can also be different depending on who, rather than what, we're trying to do.

Danica Patrick perfectly sums it up: "The best success stories are when people do what they love. Those are probably the most successful people in the world because they're willing to go the extra mile."

STANDING UP FOR WHAT'S RIGHT

DO YOU LIKE FIGHTING FOR WHAT'S RIGHT? Is it important to you to help those who are less fortunate in your community or across the globe?

If so, you're in good company! Take, for instance, **Oprah Winfrey**, who feels her work is never just about a job. She says, "Your real job is to serve something greater than yourself. No matter what you do—you're a pharmacist, a lawyer, a teacher, a mother, a doctor, a scientist, a clerk, a receptionist—how are you going to serve?" Attorney **Roberta Kaplan** worked hard to make it legal for same-sex couples to get married in the US, while civil rights activist **Diane Nash** fought racist laws and policies; their work advanced equality for all people. **Barbara Burns** broke barriers as one of America's first coal miners, and her thirteen-year battle against sexual harassment in the workplace helped give other women coal miners the courage to stand up for themselves, too.

Have you found a way to help others and make a difference, big or small? Have you thought about how to keep doing that as you grow up? These women's examples are bound to give you ideas for how to start.

★ ★ ★ ★ ★

Even though she became a huge media success, **Oprah Winfrey** didn't set out to have a career in entertainment. Growing up, she had no idea what kind of job she wanted, but she

Top: 2018 Women's March, Washington, DC; center, Barbara Burns; bottom: Gloria Steinem.

did know she wanted to do something important!

Oprah spent her early years on her grandmother's farm in rural Mississippi, without running water or electricity. She had three responsibilities: take the cows out to the pasture each morning, collect water from the pump, and deal with the "slop jar," which was for nighttime bathroom emergencies. "You tried not to have to go out to the outhouse in the middle of the night, because you never knew if there was a snake out there," remembers Oprah. "As a little kid I always thought I was going to fall through the hole." Yikes!

Oprah's grandmother never imagined that her granddaughter could be anything more than a maid. It wasn't that she didn't want Oprah to have a life full of possibilities, but opportunities for African Americans were limited in the US in the 1950s and 1960s. One day, when Oprah was about five years old, her grandmother was hanging clothes on a line and said, "Oprah Gail, you better watch me now because one day you're going to have to learn how to do this for yourself." Oprah was on the back porch churning butter, and she remembers thinking that she was going to have a different life. "I kept that whole idea to myself," she says.

In the third grade, Oprah learned an important lesson when she handed in a school book report long before it was due. Her teacher was so impressed, she shared the news with other teachers and told Oprah's classmates, "You should be more like Oprah!" This made Oprah realize something that stayed with her forever: "When you do the best that you can do, people remember you."

Oprah continued to be a go-getter as she grew older. At sixteen, she worked as a vacuum cleaner saleswoman, and by the time she was nineteen, she was on the radio. The next year, she was on TV. She worked hard, and whenever an opportunity popped up, she grabbed it. In high school, Oprah was chosen as one of two kids in her state to go to the White House Conference on Youth—a huge deal! She was interviewed on a local radio show, and eventually the host asked her if she'd audition to be Miss Fire Prevention of Nashville (someone who acts as a spokesperson for fire prevention and safety in communities). "The guy remembered me a year

> **"When you do the best that you can do, people remember you."**

The Oprah Winfrey Leadership Academy for Girls

The Oprah Winfrey Leadership Academy for Girls is a boarding school for girls in grades eight through twelve just outside of Johannesburg, South Africa. Oprah started the school after thinking hard about what would make a huge difference for girls like herself. "I know what it means to be poor," Oprah says. "I know what it feels like to be abandoned, and I know what it feels like to not be wanted. I know what it feels like to not be loved and yet have inside yourself a yearning, a passion, a desire, a hope for something better." Many of the girls at Oprah's boarding school go from living in a community where there is no water to attending universities in South Africa and the US.

later. Why? Because I was prepared, I was articulate, and I was smart," she says.

> "... I was prepared, I was articulate, and I was smart."

As Oprah pursued a career on radio and TV, she stayed focused on how she could serve others: "If I was just thinking of myself as a television reporter or an anchorwoman, I wouldn't have been able to stand it. I couldn't stand the notion of going out every day on the street and looking for the worst thing that was going to happen to people, so I had to make a shift inside myself. How am I going to use myself for something that's bigger than me?" she wondered. Soon she had her own show, then a magazine, and then a network!

Through a twenty-five-year run, *The Oprah Winfrey Show* celebrated women's experiences and gave voice to the voiceless. "What that show did was to say, 'You matter. You matter if you are a student. You matter if you have been divorced. You matter if you've been abused. You matter, no matter what your circumstances have been. You are not just circumstances.'"

▶ YOUNG & BOLD: LILLIAN PRAVDA

Lillian Pravda was born with a cataract; by the time she was five, she'd been through two surgeries to give her vision. Lillian realized that not everyone has access to the medical services she had. When she was only eight years old, she decided to start **Vision For and From Children**, an organization that raises awareness and funds to provide eye surgery and vision care for children in need. As of 2018, her organization has helped over twenty-seven thousand kids all over the world enjoy the gift of sight!

On March 27, 2013, lawyer **Roberta Kaplan** stood before the US Supreme Court to argue that same-sex couples should be given the same rights to marriage as heterosexual couples. She had fifteen minutes to make her case, and as you can imagine, she was nervous about messing up. But Roberta had trained for this and felt confident as she stood before the nine justices. She had one main goal: to ask the court to acknowledge and accept that gay people are no different from straight people and that gay people's relationships are no different from straight people's relationships. Would she be able to do it?

Long before Roberta was a lawyer standing in front of the Supreme Court, she was a little girl living in Cleveland, Ohio. When she was nine, she read her mother's copies of *New York* and *New Yorker* magazines and knew that was the city she wanted to live in. She came up with a plan: "The strategy involved going to an Ivy League college, going to law school in New York, and then moving to New York. Which, scary enough, is exactly what I did. In my whole family, I'm the only one who's ever left."

Once she started practicing as an attorney, Roberta found herself drawn to cases that made a difference to large groups of people, known as "public interest" cases. That meant her job had amazing highs and lows, from total exhilaration when she won to total anger or depression when she lost. "But there's one emotion I've never experienced for a single second at my job," Roberta adds, "which is boredom. I've never gone into the office and said to myself, 'This is very boring, what I'm doing.' And that's a huge privilege."

Roberta was on the legal team that fought for marriage equality in New York state, and even though they lost that fight, Roberta wasn't ready to give up on such an impor-

Marian Wright Edelman

When Marian Wright Edelman noticed how many children didn't have basic things like proper nutrition, health care, access to a good education, and a safe place to live, she decided to start the **Children's Defense Fund**. It was for one simple reason: "Because children needed it," Marian says. "They're the poorest group of Americans, the most neglected group of Americans, and they have no voice. They have no vote, they cannot lobby, and they are the key to America's future." The Children's Defense Fund's mission is to make sure every child gets equal opportunities through programs that provide health care, extra support at school, healthy food options, leadership training, and more.

tant issue—for all gay families and for her own as well. She and her wife were going to have a child and had gotten married in Canada, but as she explains, "The idea that we couldn't get married in our own home state . . . was very hurtful and upsetting."

Roberta knew that when you're arguing a legal case, it's better to make it about one person's story, which can represent the stories of many others. She found that with a woman named Edie Windsor. Edie and her wife, Thea Spyer, had been together for forty-four years before Thea died. Edie was asked to pay the government $600,000 in taxes on everything she inherited from Thea— a bill she wouldn't have received if she and Thea had been a heterosexual couple. Though Edie and Thea had been married in Canada, the United States did not legally recognize marriage between same-sex couples. Roberta set out to prove this was discrimination and that it violated the US Constitution.

Roberta and her team took Edie's case all the way to the Supreme Court. When they found out the court had ruled in Edie's favor in a history-making decision, it was Roberta's biggest career "high" yet. "This is going to be one of the only, if not the only, landmark Supreme Court cases where not only was the client a woman but the entire team was run by women," Roberta says of her work. "There are still plenty of mornings when I wake up and I kind of have to pinch myself. Is this really what I did?"

* * * * *

Lydia Cincore-Templeton

As a teenager, Lydia Cincore-Templeton was bullied relentlessly until her parents found her a new school where she felt safe and accepted. Since then, she's dedicated herself to helping young people who have similar struggles. In college, she studied discrimination and children's rights law. She later traveled to the Democratic Republic of Congo in Africa to help build orphanages for children who'd lost their parents to war or disease. "When we came back," Lydia remembers, "my life was changed. **I realized that someone has to speak up for the vulnerable and the voiceless here: children who are in our foster care system."** (Foster care is where adults care for kids whose birth parents aren't able to.) Lydia started the Children Youth and Family Collaborative, which provides academic and emotional support to foster kids and others at risk of not graduating high school. Now, 90 percent of students in the program get their high school diploma. Lydia is proof that sometimes hardship helps you find a greater purpose.

Rebecca Adamson

Rebecca Adamson has dedicated her life to helping indigenous people all over the world fight for their rights and autonomy. She was part of the Indian-controlled school movement in the 1970s, which **helped Native Americans create their own schools**, since students were being mistreated in mainstream schools by being taken away from their families and denied use of their own languages. Over the years, Rebecca has worked hard to pass legislation to help tribal people in the United States and all over the world achieve the power to make decisions for themselves and their communities.

You've probably heard of Martin Luther King Jr., but have you heard of **Diane Nash**? Diane was another one of the great leaders of the civil rights movement, working right alongside Dr. King to bring an end to segregation—that's a term used to describe laws and policies that unfairly separate people by race.

Diane grew up on the South Side of Chicago. Her grandmother couldn't read or write past a first-grade level and didn't believe in talking about race—she felt that made it more important than it should be. She told her granddaughter, "Don't ever let anyone mistreat you."

By 1955, a series of events made it impossible for Diane, then seventeen, not to see how much racism needed discussion—*and* action. A teenager named Emmett Till was murdered after being accused of flirting with a white woman. Later that same year, Rosa Parks and other civil rights activists launched the Montgomery bus boycott, a campaign against racial segregation on buses. Around the same time, Daisy Bates, who worked for the National Association for the Advancement of Colored People, helped integrate the Little Rock school system. A civil rights movement was growing.

When Diane arrived at college at Fisk University in Nashville, Tennessee, she wasn't prepared for daily life as an African American in the South. Her southern friends were used to things like water fountain and restroom signs that said "White" and "Colored," but they made Diane furious. She became determined to do something about segregation. Her friends tried to talk her out of getting involved, telling her, "You're not going to be successful. You're just going to get yourself in trouble." But Diane believed that laws and attitudes should—and would—change.

Diane started going to workshops on nonviolence and learned as much as she could about fighting for civil rights. Before long, she became the chairperson of the Nashville Student Central Committee. She wasn't so sure about being a leader, though. "I did not want to be chairperson. I was really, really afraid," she said. Eventually, she was persuaded to take charge and lead nonviolent demonstrations. At the time, African Americans weren't allowed to eat in downtown Nashville restaurants, which Diane found humiliating.

> **She became determined to do something about segregation. Her friends tried to talk her out of getting involved, telling her, "You're not going to be successful. You're just going to get yourself in trouble."**

She helped carefully plan peaceful "sit-ins" where blacks sat at lunch counters in restaurants, waiting to be served. They expected their opponents to say, "We don't want to sit next to dirty, smelly Negroes in the restaurants," so young men wore suits and ties and the women wore dresses. "We wanted to change people's minds and to persuade them not to be racist," Diane remembers.

During the demonstrations, Diane asked Ben West, Nashville's mayor, "Do you think it's wrong to discriminate against a person solely on the basis of their skin color?" He was forced to admit that businesses shouldn't discriminate, which was a radical, momentous response at the time. The next day, the city newspaper's headline was: "Integrate Counters— Mayor." Within a few weeks, Nashville became the first southern city to officially desegregate its lunch counters. That would be the first of many missions accomplished for Diane, including the Freedom Rides and the 1963 March on Washington.

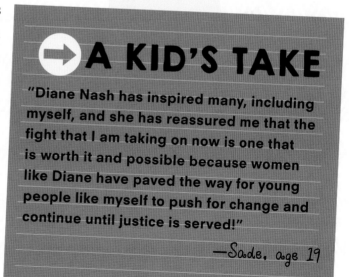

→ **A KID'S TAKE**

"Diane Nash has inspired many, including myself, and she has reassured me that the fight that I am taking on now is one that is worth it and possible because women like Diane have paved the way for young people like myself to push for change and continue until justice is served!"

—Sade, age 19

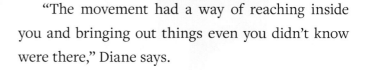

MARCHES

Big public marches are a way for people to make their voices heard about a certain issue. Have you ever marched for something? In January 2017, **over seven million people of all ages around the world marched in the name of Women's Rights**, and in March 2018, nearly two million took part in the student-led March for Our Lives to demand tighter gun control laws. One of the most famous marches of the women's movement took place on August 26, 1970, on the fiftieth anniversary of the women's suffrage amendment. Marches prove to us that when we fight for a cause, we don't have to do it alone, and together we can help bring change.

"The movement had a way of reaching inside you and bringing out things even you didn't know were there," Diane says.

★ ★ ★ ★ ★

In the 1980s, **Barbara Burns** became one of America's first female coal miners, breaking new ground for all women in a way she didn't expect.

Barbara grew up in West Virginia, where most of her male family members were coal miners. "When I was about eight years old," she remembers, "I thought, I do not want to be like my mom. We couldn't do anything except clean house, cook, and things like that." Instead, Barbara wanted to be a nurse. To earn money for nursing school, she started working at the coal mines. She'd never seen any female miners before, but she knew there was a women's movement happening in the US. "That's what really prompted me to apply for the job in the mines," Barbara says.

Something surprising happened: Barbara discovered that she loved coal mining. Eventually, she was offered a job as safety director at a big coal mining company. "I took my job very, very seriously . . . doing what was necessary

"We couldn't do anything except clean house, cook, and things like that."

YOUNG & BOLD: NAOMI WADLER

Naomi Wadler was eleven years old when she spoke at the March for Our Lives in Washington, DC, in 2017. It was a rally that called for stricter gun laws and restrictions intended to help reduce gun violence. Statistically, gun violence disproportionately affects black women and girls. **"I am here to acknowledge and represent the African American girls whose stories don't make the front page of every national newspaper,"** Naomi said. "I represent the African American women who are victims of gun violence, who are simply statistics instead of vibrant, beautiful girls full of potential. For far too long, these names, these black girls and women, have been just numbers. I'm here to say 'Never again.'"

to keep the men from being in danger." But Barbara's boss had other ideas for what her "job" should be, telling her that if he wanted to kiss or hug his employees, he would. She told him, "Nobody kisses me unless I want them to." Still, Barbara's boss continued to bother her, trying to get her to date him even though she asked him over and over again to stop. That's not just inappropriate—it's illegal.

At first, Barbara worried that if she complained to someone, she'd lose the job she loved. When Barbara couldn't take it anymore, she hired an attorney and filed a complaint against her company with the West Virginia Commission on Human Rights in 1986, stating that she'd experienced sexual harassment. It took fourteen years, but the court finally ruled in Barbara's favor.

Gloria Steinem

Gloria Steinem was a reporter and magazine columnist in the 1960s, covering stories about women's issues, when she had a major aha moment after attending a speak-out and hearing women tell the truth about their lives: **she realized that men's lives and experiences were taken seriously, but women's were not.** She quickly became a leading activist and advocate for women's rights and equality. She remembers thinking, "These injustices are so great, surely if we just explain them to people, they will want to fix them." That was, well, not so easy . . . but when Gloria helped found *Ms.* magazine, it was clear there was an audience for serious stories about women's lives: the first issue sold out in eight days! Since then, Gloria's dedicated her life to fighting for women's rights and equality, traveling the world speaking to and organizing groups that are working to make lasting change in their communities.

Barbara won legally, but another victory came outside the courtroom: after Barbara spoke out, female colleagues came forward with their own experiences, and coal companies became aware of what sexual harassment in the workplace actually was. "This case being made public really helped other women," Barbara says. "And it was worth it."

➡️ A KID'S TAKE

"Barbara Burns stood up and persevered in the case against Smoot Coal. It really struck me how she went through all those terrible things, but she found the courage to get help and file a lawsuit. She also did something that she enjoyed that other women at the time didn't do, breaking stereotypes by becoming a coal miner." —Dilara, age 12

★ ★ ★ ★ ★

So . . . what causes do *you* care about? What are you willing to fight for?

Anti-bullying? Saving the environment? Animal rights? Taking a stand against racism, sexism, violence, or negative media messages? Maybe your family has a

THE WOMEN'S MOVEMENT

When people talk about "the women's movement," they're usually referring to a phase of American history in the 1960s and 1970s when massive strides were made toward equality. Sometimes it's called "the feminist movement," "the women's liberation movement," or "another civil rights movement." Activists in the movement pushed for women's equal rights in lots of different ways, such as fighting for new laws and policies, raising people's awareness of issues that affect women, creating organizations to support women, encouraging the media to represent women realistically, and more. Screenwriter, producer, and director **Diane English** describes the women's movement as **"the biggest social movement in the history of the planet earth, because it affected everybody."** Since then, there have been different waves of the women's movement, and it continues today.

certain cause that's important to all of you, or a recent news story has gotten you fired up. Keep in mind that anything big or small can make a difference, from running a lemonade stand to raise money for a cause to writing letters to elected officials.

As US Representative Val Demings says: "If you don't like something, then you do something to change it. Every individual

> ## "If you don't like something, then you do something to change it.

living in this country has an opportunity—an obligation—to make their community, their state, this nation better."

And remember that activism is contagious (in a totally good way): when you work to make a difference, you inspire others to do the same.

The Equal Rights Amendment

The Equal Rights Amendment (ERA) was first introduced to the US Congress in 1923. It says: **"Equality of rights under the law shall not be denied or abridged by the United States or by any state on account of sex."** The ERA hasn't yet been ratified (been officially accepted), though it is introduced every year. In the 1970s and '80s, Phyllis Schlafly, a conservative activist and founder of the Eagle Forum, mobilized people to defeat the ERA. She erroneously argued that the ERA meant women would be drafted into the military and that bathrooms would have to be gender neutral. Even though the ERA hasn't passed, today the frontline military is open to women, and many bathrooms are gender neutral.

7

SHATTERING STEREOTYPES

HAVE YOU EVER FELT like someone stereotyped you, or that you stereotyped someone? A stereotype is a belief you might have about a group of people, or a way to judge them, based on what you've heard or seen. Usually, stereotypes are negative and untrue. An example of a stereotype might be someone saying, "Short kids aren't as good at sports as taller kids" or "Girls like pink and boys like blue."

The women in this chapter are great examples of shattering stereotypes. **Lena Waithe** was the first black lesbian to win an Emmy in writing, a category often filled with white men. CEO **Anne Wojcicki** pursued a career in science with few female role models to help her carve her path. Civil rights activist **Aileen Hernandez**'s mother was determined not to let her children be treated differently from anyone else. Aileen took careful note, and it's no surprise that she ended up in a career dedicated to helping people challenge unfairness in their lives. **Maya Lin** pursued architecture at a time when less than 10 percent of architects were female. Former secretary of state **Condoleezza Rice** grew up in segregated Alabama in the 1960s but had support at home to know that she could accomplish more than society expected. She says, "My parents had me absolutely convinced that even if I couldn't have a hamburger at the Woolworth's lunch counter, I could be president of the United States if I wanted to be."

Top: Reshma Saujani; center, left: Ayanna Howard; center, right: Aileen Hernandez; bottom: Marie Curie.

Luckily, the women in this chapter are each expanding our understanding of what people can do—and be.

★ ★ ★ ★ ★

"The things that make us different—those are our superpowers!"

That's what writer, actor, and producer **Lena Waithe** told the audience when she accepted her Emmy Award for Outstanding Writing for a Comedy Series in 2017 for her work on the Netflix series *Master of None*. She was the first African American woman to win in that category. Lena's words reminded the cheering crowd that the things that make us different might actually lead us to creating great stuff in life.

Lena was raised on the South Side of Chicago in a house full of women, including her mother and grandmother. She was inspired by how they all have "a lot of strength, a lot of pride, a lot of integrity, and there's also a nice amount of sass and swag, too." Lena loved watching TV shows like *The Cosby Show*, *A Different World*, and *The Fresh Prince of Bel-Air*, and she felt connected to the characters. By the time she graduated high school, Lena knew she wanted to write for television and so went on to study cinema and television arts in college.

> **"The things that make us different— those are our superpowers!"**

After moving to Los Angeles, Lena worked hard as an assistant for several TV and film producers, including Ava DuVernay (read about her in chapter 8). She says her secret to getting hired again and again was being the most excited person on set. "There [was] nothing that I would say no to doing," says Lena. Eventually Lena started writing her own scripts and got hired as a writer for the Nickelodeon show *How to Rock*. Then a casting director suggested that Lena audition for acting roles.

Lena got cast as Denise in *Master of None*. Her character was originally supposed to be a white woman, but the producers, comedian Aziz Ansari and his partner Alan Yang, decided to change the character to be not just black but also gay—like Lena. "You're definitely not what we had in mind," Lena remembers them saying, "but you're a lot more interesting than what we could've ever come up with, and so we're going to run with it."

One day, Lena shared with them the story of how she told her mother she was gay. Aziz and Alan asked her to help them turn it into an episode about Denise, which won her that groundbreaking Emmy Award. After working on *Master of None*, Lena appeared in films like *Ready Player One*, and she writes and produces the Showtime series *The Chi*, about the South Side of Chicago, long known as one of the roughest neighborhoods. "There's a lot of storytellers that don't look like the storytellers of yesteryear, you know," says Lena. "I think we're just being ourselves and expressing ourselves and figuring out new and different ways to put art out into the world."

Breaking Stereotypes on TV

In the past, female characters on television were usually wives, mothers, or girlfriends. Eventually, there were a few female characters who were single, had careers, or were on their own journey in some other way that wasn't all about a guy. If there hadn't been shows with female main characters like those featured in *That Girl*, created by Marlo Thomas in the 1960s, there might not have been *Murphy Brown*, created by Diane English in the 1980s—or even *The Unbreakable Kimmy Schmidt* decades later. Who will today's great characters inspire tomorrow?

1966: **That Girl**

1968: **Julia**

1970: **The Mary Tyler Moore Show**

1972: **Maude**

1988: **Murphy Brown**

2015: **The Unbreakable Kimmy Schmidt**

Geena Davis Institute on Gender in Media

The Oscars—awards given for cinematic work, also known as the Academy Awards—have pretty much been a white-guy thing: **a 2012 report on Oscar voters** (professionals from the film industry) **revealed that 94 percent were white and 77 percent were male.** With increasing pressure to diversify Hollywood, those numbers are beginning to shift. Actress Geena Davis created the Geena Davis Institute on Gender in Media, to help raise awareness of how women are represented on camera and behind the scenes in the entertainment industry. Change does happen! In 2017, 39 percent of the Academy of Motion Picture Art and Sciences' *new* members were women, and 30 percent were people of color. The 2018 Best Director nominees included a woman for the first time in five years (Greta Gerwig for *Lady Bird*) as well as an African American man (Jordan Peele for *Get Out*).

Anne Wojcicki grew up in Northern California in the '70s and '80s as the youngest of three girls. Her parents were both teachers and raised their daughters to believe they could do anything they wanted. "There was never a sense of 'You're a girl and this is what you should do' and 'You're a boy and this is what you should do,'" Anne remembers. When her sisters weren't bothering her, she was "sort of ignored," which Anne later realized was a big advantage. When you're the youngest, she says, "You learn how to effectively get what you need but not to rely on other people to actually give you lots of things."

When Anne was six, she heard her mother telling her sister that something was "in your genes." Anne was confused, because her sister wasn't wearing *jeans*! Her mom explained that genes are part of your body's makeup and help determine characteristics of who you are. That year, a chemistry set was waiting under the Christmas tree for Anne, and since then, she's been fascinated by science.

When she was in fourth grade, Anne made a magnet out of a Styrofoam cup and showed it to her dad's class of Stanford University students. After the class, she thought: "I'm only in the fourth grade, and I'm as capable as these Stanford kids." But when Anne went to

GIRLS WHO CODE

Reshma Saujani doesn't take no for an answer! She applied to Yale Law School three times before she was accepted and has run for citywide office twice (though she hasn't won . . . yet). She's also the founder of the organization Girls Who Code. Reshma got tired of seeing how coding—designing and building computer programs and mobile apps—was mostly done by boys. She wanted to crack that stereotype and give all girls, especially those with less access to computers and tech training, the tools they need to be part of the coding world. So far, girls have created codes to make games, help monitor cancer, and more. If you could make your own game or app, what would it be?

Megan Smith

In 2014, President Obama appointed Megan Smith to the position of chief technology officer to the US government. As a kid, Megan loved science and math. She studied engineering in college and spent many years working at Google. She has a great passion for STEAM— science, technology, engineering, arts, and math. Megan feels that one of the best ways to motivate women and girls into STEAM careers is to show them how other women are making an impact in these fields. **"We need to know that women have always done these [technology] jobs, even if they've been written out of the stories,"** she says. "Kids have to understand how to be not just consumers of technology, but makers!"

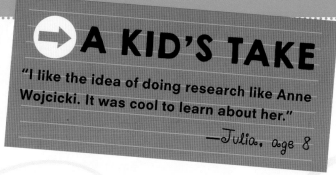

A KID'S TAKE

"I like the idea of doing research like Anne Wojcicki. It was cool to learn about her."

—Julia, age 8

college, things changed. For the first time, she felt judged for being a woman and that certain opportunities weren't available to her. Still, she followed her passions. She considered majoring in physics or Russian literature, but in the end she chose biology.

After college, Anne became a health care analyst—that's someone who researches and studies medical data. It was a field where there weren't many women. "I'd go to conferences where it was all men in suits," Anne remembers. "One upside was you never had to wait for the bathroom!" She enjoyed her work, but after she began volunteering at Bellevue Hospital, a public hospital in New York City, she realized what she really wanted to do in her career was help people.

Her volunteer work at the hospital also got Anne thinking about how our bodies are all different on the inside: Why do some people respond better to a certain medicine than others? Why is a disease more likely to affect one person than another? In 2006, she cofounded 23andMe, a company that provides kits for people to send in a sample of their own DNA (in the form of saliva) and get a full report on what it says about their health, their traits, and even their ancestry. The name comes from the fact that human DNA is made up of twenty-three pairs of chromosomes.

To date, Anne's company has over five million customers and has published research on diseases like Parkinson's and breast cancer. "Even if it's unsuccessful, going through

Ayanna Howard

Ayanna Howard never lost sight of her childhood dream to build robots. She got a degree in artificial intelligence and then started working for NASA. She was a young African American woman put in charge of older engineers who were all men. One of them thought she was a secretary. Ayanna combated these assumptions and used her own example to push past people's limited understanding of what women could accomplish. "I spoke up and didn't sit down," Ayanna says. **"Keep proving yourself, because you're awesome."** With Ayanna as their leader, her team eventually developed the artificial intelligence for Mars rovers. Today, she runs her own company creating robotic tools for kids with special needs.

that process of being with a team of people who are all trying to create something is phenomenal," Anne says. "You have to wake up and do something every day. So you might as well do what you love, and you might as well try to have an impact."

> **"You have to wake up and do something every day. So you might as well do what you love, and you might as well try to have an impact."**

* * * * *

Aileen Hernandez was a first at many things: she was the first woman appointed to the Equal Employment Opportunity Commission (see chapter 2), and she was a founding member of the National Organization for Women. Her parents immigrated to the United States from Jamaica and initially settled in Harlem because, Aileen says, "That's where you went as an African American." In the 1930s, the family moved to Brooklyn, where neighbors started a petition trying to get them to leave because "they didn't want black people to be in the neighborhood."

Aileen's mother took her and walked over to the house of the family who started the petition, demanding to speak with the husband. She walked in, knocked off the man's hat, and said: "When I'm talking to you, I want you to look at me . . ." then gave him a piece of her mind. When the elementary school principal heard what had happened, he called a parents' meeting to tell everyone: "I want you to know that if you don't let [Aileen's family] live in [their] house, I will give them my house to live in."

That day, Aileen learned a valuable lesson about stereotypes: "There are all kinds of

THE MADAME CURIE COMPLEX

Women's contributions to science often aren't known or credited; this is called the Madame Curie Complex. The lopsided recognition of men versus women in the sciences can be seen using just one example—the Nobel Prize, an award given to people who excel in the sciences, among other fields. **As of 2017, only forty-eight women have been awarded a Nobel Prize** (Marie Curie, a European scientist who discovered radium and polonium, won twice), compared to 844 men.

people and all kinds of communities, so you can't decide that because you had a bad situation with one person of a certain ethnicity from then on everybody in that ethnicity has to be knocked out."

Aileen loved school. In the 1940s, she got a full scholarship to Howard University, a historically black college in Washington, DC. Aileen had experienced discrimination before but was surprised that the nation's capital was completely segregated. When she was told to get into the line for a "black cab," she assumed that meant the color of the cab, not the color of her skin!

At college, Aileen signed up for an international government class where she was the only girl. On the first day of class, the professor suggested that Aileen might instead sign up for home economics, a class for women to learn skills like sewing, cooking, and taking care of children. Aileen thought about leaving the international government class, but then stayed. "I knew my mother would

> **At college, Aileen signed up for an international government class where she was the only girl.**

never forgive me if I [left]," she says. Aileen ended up proving herself so well in that class, her professor invited her to do a special project studying how many black people were in government jobs above a certain level (which, at the time, of course, was not many).

After college, Aileen set off on her career, first as an organizer with the International

Ladies Garment Workers Union (ILGWU). She talked to bosses to make sure they knew what their workers' rights were. Then she worked with many groups making sure that companies weren't discriminating against employees. Once the Civil Rights Act of 1964 passed, there was a national five-person commission set up to enforce the new antidiscrimination legislation. "I got appointed to the commission because I actually met all of the requirements and all in one person. I was a woman, I was an African American, I had a last name of Hernandez, so I'm also Latino." The other four members were men!

Where did Aileen get the strength to succeed in difficult environments? "I was always told when I was growing up that I had choices," Aileen says. "Even when really I didn't have a whole lot of them at that time. If I wanted my life to go a certain way, I had to stand up for things that I believed in."

"If I wanted my life to go a certain way, I had to stand up for things that I believed in."

★ ★ ★ ★ ★

THE FEMININE MYSTIQUE

In the 1950s, writer **Betty Friedan** sent a questionnaire to her former college classmates, asking them if they felt satisfied with their lives. Turns out, most were unhappy and believed they weren't living up to their potential. Betty called this "the feminine mystique," and in 1963 she wrote a book with that title. As Betty described it: "The feminine mystique had made women feel it's unfeminine to use our rights, to want equality, to want to take part in the decisions of the world in politics." *The Feminine Mystique* became a bestseller and helped spark the feminist movement in the US, inspiring women across America to rethink their life goals and try to make their mark in some fulfilling way. After the success of *The Feminine Mystique*, Betty and others launched the National Organization for Women, which continues to advocate for laws that help women reach their full potential.

In 1980, **Maya Lin** was a senior in college, majoring in architecture. A classmate saw a poster announcing a competition for designs for the Vietnam Veterans Memorial, which was to be built in Washington, DC. Some of Maya's classmates decided to create their own competition for the memorial. A few months later, Maya submitted her design to the real competition . . . and won. The competition entries were kept anonymous, so Maya will always wonder: Would she still have won if the committee had known that she was a young Asian American woman?

Maya's plan for the Vietnam Veterans Memorial was to cut into the earth and open it up, building two long, black granite walls engraved with the names of the more than fifty-eight thousand servicemen and servicewomen who died or went missing in the Vietnam War. The walls are polished so people can see their own reflection when they look at the names; Maya's design focused on creating more acceptance about those who had been lost and the sacrifices they made. "I had an inclination that we needed to be honest about the loss," says Maya. "I was beginning to explore how architecture has an impact on us from a physiological point of view and from a political point of view." After three years of controversy and delays—many people felt the design looked like a "black scar"—the memorial was finally built in 1982.

Years earlier, when Maya was a freshman in college, she wondered: What am I going to do with the rest of my life? She considered architecture because it was a combination of math and art, two subjects she loved. But when she visited the architecture department, the director told her: "Come back in two years. We don't take people into the major until you've gotten a well-grounded approach." Maya didn't let that discourage her. She studied everything she could, and at the end of her sophomore year, she went back and announced: "I'm ready."

★　★　★　★　★

"I was beginning to explore how architecture has an impact on us from a physiological point of view and from a political point of view."

Majora Carter

Majora Carter is passionate about helping communities reach their full potential. Majora grew up in the Bronx in the 1970s. At that time, people often heard the phrase "The Bronx is burning" because landlords sometimes burned buildings instead of improving them. "I spent most of my formative years feeling the stain associated with being from a place where everybody assumed nothing good could come out of it," Majora says. But when she noticed that people in her community were getting sick because of pollution, she decided to do something about it. **She started a program that helped people coming out of prison get training in "green" fields** like urban forestry (taking care of trees and plants in cities) and installing environmentally friendly roofs. It was a great way to empower people with important skills and help the neighborhood at the same time.

→ A KID'S TAKE

"Majora Carter is inspiring. To have such determination in tackling the stigma of the Bronx, and working to try and make it better, makes her a force to be reckoned with. She's truly someone worth looking up to."

—Calayah Bah, age 18

As a child, former US secretary of state **Condoleezza Rice** was convinced she'd grow up to be a concert pianist. She learned piano from her grandmother, and by the time she was four years old she was already performing in concerts. That dream was shattered fifteen years later, when Condoleezza attended summer school at the Aspen Music Festival and met musicians who were much younger but had more ability than her. She went back to college desperate to find a new major.

After a couple of false starts, Condoleezza wandered into a course in international politics taught by an expert on Russia named Josef Korbel (who, coincidentally, was the father of Madeleine Albright, who would become the first female secretary of state under President Bill Clinton). "Josef Korbel opened up this world to me of diplomacy and international politics and things Russian," Condoleezza remembers. "All of a sudden I knew I wanted to study the Soviet Union."

One of Condoleezza's first jobs was in the arms control and disarmament program at Stanford University. "We probably were the only four women in the country working in this very male-dominated field, but here we were all together," she says of her three female coworkers. Eventually, she became a professor at Stanford, and her expertise on Russia became well known. In 1989 she was invited to work for the National Security Council under President George H. W. Bush, and then again in 2000 under his son, President George W. Bush.

On September 11, 2001, Condoleezza was at her desk having a normal morning at work when an assistant told her about a first—and then a second—plane crashing into the World Trade Center towers in New York City. She knew it was a terrorist attack, and she knew how the US government should react. "I always knew that the most important thing to do after the attack was to put emphasis again on diplomacy," she says.

Moments after President Bush's reelection three years later, he asked Condoleezza to become his secretary of state. It would be an incredible job but also a huge responsibility. It took her a few days to say yes (much like it took Hillary Clinton some convincing—see chapter 4).

Even though she gave up being a professional musician, Condoleezza still loves music, from Led Zeppelin to Kool & the Gang to Brahms and Mozart. She's also knowledgeable

▶ THE BOMBING OF THE 16TH STREET BAPTIST CHURCH

One of the many turning points in the civil rights movement was the September 15, 1963, bombing of the 16th Street Baptist Church in Birmingham, Alabama. The bomb had been planted by members of the Ku Klux Klan (a secret society organized in the South after the Civil War that believes in white supremacy; the KKK is still in existence today). That morning, Condoleezza Rice was with her family at a nearby church where her father was a minister. "We heard the bomb go off, and we actually felt it," Condoleezza remembers. "Birmingham had come to be known as *Bombingham,* and bombs going off in neighborhoods was an almost daily occurrence. I remember as a child just not understanding how people could hate us that much and for the first time really being pretty scared."

WOMEN'S AND CIVIL RIGHTS

The fight for women's rights and the fight for civil rights are often treated as two different movements, but for many people—especially women of color—you can't distinguish discrimination based on gender from discrimination based on race. **"I was very aware of the twin movements for the empowerment and justice for black citizens, which frankly impacted our lives more than the second great movement, which was the women's movement,"** Condoleezza Rice says. "If you were black in Birmingham and you were a little girl who loved to play the piano, and you could suddenly go to the Birmingham-Southern Conservatory of Music in 1964, that meant a lot."

about sports, which has come in handy when trying to get along with male coworkers. Condoleezza did other things that challenged gender stereotypes. During her first day at the Pentagon, one of her male colleagues said: "The rookie makes the coffee." Condoleezza made the coffee so strong, her male colleagues never asked her to make the coffee again.

For Condoleezza, there was a simple solution to pushing through other people's stereotypes: "I had a Russian general say to me once, 'Why's a nice girl like you interested in these military affairs?' But over time, you realize that if you become known as capable at what you're doing, those prejudices tend to go away."

"If you were black in Birmingham and you were a little girl who loved to play the piano, and you could suddenly go to the Birmingham-Southern Conservatory of Music in 1964, that meant a lot."

* * * * *

What is "Feminism"?

For many people, feminism is a movement that gives them confidence and guidance as they balance their personal and professional lives. How each person defines "feminism" can differ, from changing laws to changing attitudes so everyone can thrive in the ways they should.

Valerie Jarrett ➡ former senior advisor to President Barack Obama:

> **"I think feminism is about making sure women can thrive, and where gender is not the issue that defines whether or not you're going to be successful."**

Elizabeth Blackburn ➡ Nobel Prize–winning biologist:

> **"Feminism is about people living to their full potential. I think that's the minimum that anybody should ask."**

Ruth Simmons ➡ university president:

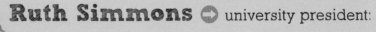

> **"Feminism has to do with consciousness. If you are a feminist you cannot sit still when you know that people are treating women unjustly."**

Ruth Bader Ginsburg → Supreme Court justice:

"People say 'feminism' is a dirty word because they don't understand what it means. The simplest explanation is the notion that we should each be free to develop all our talents, whatever they may be, and not be held back by artificial barriers. These are manmade barriers, certainly not heaven-sent."

Shonda Rhimes → screenwriter and producer:

"I'm not sure why 'feminist' would be a dirty word. It's actually kind of a very strong, interesting, and clean word. It always makes me sad when someone tries to make themselves smaller to be less threatening."

Eleanor Holmes Norton → US congresswoman:

"I learned to be a feminist by being denied my rights as an African American. Over time it became absolutely clear, it wasn't a moment in time; what had begun with the right to vote had never been finished."

Ursula Burns → former CEO of Xerox:

"Absolutely I'm a feminist. I think women are different than men and that's a good thing and the differences between women and men should be celebrated."

Has someone ever assumed you could or couldn't do something, based on your gender, ethnicity, or how you look? It's probably happened to all of us, whether or not we know it. That's why books like this are important: we can see that women from all backgrounds and with all different kinds of experiences can do anything they set their mind to.

There are small ways we can fight stereotypes every day. Speak up when you hear someone attempting to limit or minimize others. If you see TV shows or movies that portray people in narrow roles, point it out to your friends and family; maybe write a review or article about it. Or use social media to call people out on how misguided they are!

Most importantly, pay attention to how you may be stereotyping others without realizing it. Remember to see people not as groups but as individuals, who, like Lena Waithe says, each have their own superpowers!

DREAM BIG!

YOU: "OMG, I JUST had the most amazing idea! It's going to be awesome!"

You, five seconds later: "There's no way I can do that."

Sound familiar? If so, you're not alone. We all have doubts about what we can achieve. Many times we talk ourselves out of even trying in the first place.

But what happens if we just go for it? Here are some women who did.

Champion basketball player **Lisa Leslie** tried out for basketball even though she didn't know anything about it, and she became a top professional player. When she was a kid, **Marin Alsop** was told that women couldn't be conductors, and yet she became the first female conductor of a major orchestra. **Ava DuVernay** didn't go to film school, but when she started working in Hollywood, she didn't think there was any reason why she couldn't make a movie of her own.

Hopefully these stories will inspire you to take your big dreams and make them a reality.

★ ★ ★ ★ ★

Starting in ninth grade, future basketball star **Lisa Leslie** set short- and long-term goals for herself:

▶ **Be an Olympian**

▶ **Win MVP (most valuable player)**

▶ **Get a scholarship to college**

Top: Camryn Cowan; center: Lisa Leslie and the US Women's Basketball Team; bottom, left: Chely Wright; bottom, right: Ava DuVernay.

- ▶ **Win an NCAA (National Collegiate Athletic Association) championship**
- ▶ **Dunk a basketball**

Lisa ended up checking (almost) all these things off her list . . . she didn't win an NCAA championship. But she can add to the list other awesome achievements, like being a model and broadcaster. Moral of Lisa's story: make goals!

Lisa grew up in Compton, California (where tennis stars Serena and Venus Williams are from, too), the middle child of three daughters. Her mom was a single parent who had many jobs, like being a welder, mail carrier, and truck driver. Even though she worked in typically masculine jobs, she embraced being feminine—Lisa remembers her mother's beautiful skin and that she always wore lipstick and nail polish. "She set an amazing example that you can do anything," Lisa says.

Compton was considered a "bad" neighborhood, but Lisa didn't agree. She loved playing Double Dutch, kickball, and tetherball on the street with other neighborhood kids. By the time she was in sixth grade, Lisa was six feet tall and wore a size twelve shoe. In seventh grade, a classmate told her she should try out for the basketball team. Lisa had never played basketball, but she tried out anyway and made the team. "That's really where my life completely changed," Lisa says.

At first, Lisa didn't exactly kill it on the court. But she was good at listening to feedback and improving. For a long time, she played on boys' teams because there weren't many girls' basketball teams. "I remember they kept saying, 'Give it to the girl,'" Lisa says. When she was eighteen, she was offered a full scholarship to the University of Southern California.

Once she started playing seriously, she realized there were always going to be players trying to be better than her. "That was my moment when I realized I should never say that I'm good or I'm the best. I'm always a work in progress," she says. Lisa tried out for the 1992 Olympic team and made

> **"That was my moment when I realized I should never say that I'm good or I'm the best. I'm always a work in progress."**

The Women's National Basketball Association

You've probably heard of the New York Knicks and the Miami Heat or about male basketball players like LeBron James and Michael Jordan. Have you also heard of the Phoenix Mercury and the Los Angeles Sparks or Sheryl Swoopes and Teresa Weatherspoon? These women's teams and players are part of the Women's National Basketball Association (WNBA), which was started in 1997. **By 2015, the WNBA had twelve teams across the United States.** Lisa Leslie says this about women's basketball: "The numbers don't lie; women shoot a higher percentage, whether it's field goal percentage, whether it's free throw percentage, three-point field goal percentage, our rebounding percentages." And it's not just women paying attention. "There are a lot of NBA guys that are true WNBA fans. They come out and watch us, they support us, they know the stats," says Lisa. "I think more men are finding it more acceptable to be fans of the women's game."

it to the final round, but then got cut. "I think it's those times when you get cut that it really builds character. You know, you cry for a little bit, but you get back up," she says.

And she absolutely did: Lisa eventually made the next Olympic team and won the gold medal. She remembers it well: "In 1996 in Atlanta, Georgia, in front of our USA crowd. Thirty-five thousand people chanting, 'USA.' It really is an amazing experience. When I got my gold medal, I really thought it was the last day I was going to ever play basketball."

Then, a few years after Lisa graduated from college, something amazing happened: the WNBA (Women's National Basketball Association) was created. Lisa became one of the league's top players and was the first to dunk a ball in a game—a move that most people thought only male players could pull off.

"I believe in a quote that says, 'Life is

Violet Palmer

"I was so scared." That's how Violet Palmer felt when she stepped onto the basketball court in 1997 to become the first woman to referee in the National Basketball Association (NBA) *and* the first female official in any major US professional sport. She got a lot of pushback from players at first, but eventually they supported her. **"I was given the respect as a woman, but I earned the respect as a referee,"** says Violet. And she has these words of wisdom for anyone who has ever been told they can't do something: "If I had taken that, I wouldn't be an NBA referee."

a competition, so compete,'" Lisa explains. "It's important to be competitive because we are competitive as children—we compete in sports, we compete in school; you want to get the best grades. We compete to go to college. I think that 'competition' is a healthy word that we need to sort of change our mindsets about and encourage our kids to be competitive, because life is really a competition."

* * * * *

Marin Alsop had her own big dreams growing up. Both her parents were professional musicians, so it's no surprise that Marin followed in their footsteps and became the first woman to conduct a major orchestra (a conductor directs a musical performance the way a stage director directs a play). But it also made for a pretty unusual childhood. "Our days were defined by what [performing] gigs my parents had," says Marin. "Every evening, my parents went to work when everyone else's family came home."

Living in such a creative environment, Marin always had the sense that nothing was out of reach—if you got an idea, all you had to do was start working toward it.

Marin started playing piano when she was two and violin when she was about five. When she was nine, Marin went to New York City with her dad to see Leonard Bernstein perform (he's often described as one of the best conductors of all time). Marin didn't know who he was, but she was impressed with his animated conducting style—he'd sometimes turn to the audience, and Marin was convinced he was looking right

Vivian Stringer

Vivian Stringer began her teaching and basketball coaching career in the early 1970s at a small historically black college outside of Philadelphia. For Vivian, success has never been about wins or losses. "It's measured more by where you were and where you are now," says Vivian. She has coached her teams to multiple women's championships. **"I want every woman to know that she's just as good as the guys.** It doesn't matter that there are fifteen or twenty thousand people coming to the men's games," says Vivian. "No one can ever make you feel inferior unless you allow that."

YOUNG & BOLD: CAMRYN COWAN AND JORDAN MILLAR

Camryn Cowan and Jordan Millar were only eleven years old when music they composed, "Harlem Shake" and "Boogie Down Uptown," was performed by the New York Philharmonic—to a standing ovation. "We all have our own stories to tell, so why not express them through music?" says Jordan. Camryn and Jordan were part of the Philharmonic's Very Young Composers initiative, a program that partners with schools in New York City to teach students how to compose music and then workshops their pieces. "I think I have more things ahead of me," says Camryn. "I hope that I will continue doing what I love, which is making music."

"I think I have more things ahead of me. . . . I hope that I will continue doing what I love, which is making music."

at her! "That's the day I decided I must be a conductor," Marin says. (Fun fact: years later, Marin got to work with Leonard Bernstein, and she remembers it as an epic experience: "I think it's rare to have a hero, and I think it's very rare to have that hero exceed one's expectations.")

Marin's parents were thrilled by their daughter's ambition to become a conductor, but her teacher wasn't as enthusiastic. Her teacher even tried to steer Marin in another direction. "She told me that 'Well, conductors . . . You know you're too young to be a conductor. And girls don't do that,'" Marin recalls. She was devastated. "I never even considered this possibility. I really had never considered that girls couldn't do something." That's when Marin started noticing the lack of women in leadership roles in the music world.

Though her teacher's attitude might have made some people give up, it didn't stop Marin. "I never doubted that I would achieve my goal of becoming a conductor," she says.

In college, she was already training for her future profession. She would invite her friends over to dinner, and after eating, she would have them play music while she conducted them.

In 2007, Marin became the conductor of the Baltimore Symphony Orchestra. She's very proud of that accomplishment, but also finds it a bit sad. "How can we be in the twenty-first century and there can still be firsts for women?"

> ## "How can we be in the twenty-first century and there can still be firsts for women?"

Tavi Gevinson

When Tavi Gevinson was eleven years old, she thought it would be fun to create a blog for kids and teens where she would talk about clothes, accessories, and relatable issues like popularity and bullying. She called it *Style Rookie*. When she was fifteen, she wrote on her blog about wanting to expand her blog into an online magazine, and how she was inspired by Jane Pratt's famed magazine *Sassy*. Jane read her post and offered to help Tavi. In *Rookie,* Tavi featured stories from readers, and when she asked people to submit their writing or photos, she got over three thousand submissions, including some heart-wrenching letters from readers. "We had a post about when you first start noticing other people noticing your bodies—mostly men," says Tavi. "The responses to that were really crazy, because it's something that every girl goes through." Tavi learned how important it is for young people to be able to express anger, instead of ignoring it or keeping it inside. Tavi noticed that if you're a girl, you're taught not to get in other people's way. Tavi takes a different attitude. She says: **"I don't like to apologize for things that shouldn't be apologized for."**

Marin wants to create opportunities for women in music and wants orchestras to better reflect the diversity of our communities. To help, she's created a music after-school program for kids in West Baltimore who otherwise wouldn't have access to musical instruments. "I'm hoping in ten, twenty years we'll see a lot of these kids in our major orchestras," Marin says.

⋆ ⋆ ⋆ ⋆ ⋆

When filmmaker **Ava DuVernay** was a young girl, she saw the classic movie musical *West Side Story*, and it changed her life. She loved how colorful and romantic it was, but mostly she loved all the "brown" people. "They were like the people in my neighborhood," remembers Ava, who grew up in the Los Angeles neighborhood of Compton, California. (Yep, just like Lisa Leslie and the Williams sisters.)

Once Ava was out of school, she pursued her passion for broadcast journalism and got an internship at CBS Evening News. Then she spent fourteen years doing publicity for films, which gave her a close-up look at what goes into making a movie. Ava realized: I can do that!

Ava started small, producing a couple of short films, then went bigger and used $50,000 of her own savings to make her first feature-length fiction film, *I Will Follow*. The famous movie critic Roger Ebert gave it a rave review, calling it "one of the best films I've seen about the loss of a loved one." Ava built on that success to make her next film, *Middle of Nowhere*, and went on to win an award for Best Director at the Sundance Film Festival—the first African American woman ever to do that.

In 2016, Ava was offered the chance to direct the film version of one of the most-loved children's books ever: the science-fiction classic *A Wrinkle in Time*. This made Ava the first woman of color ever to direct a film with a budget over $100 million. She put her own spin on the story, casting the main character's family as biracial, and the movie was praised for the way it celebrates female empowerment and diversity.

As Ava continues to put her ideas on the big screen, she works to make sure other women have platforms to tell their stories, too. "You have to start somewhere, and then momentum takes over," says Ava. "Before long, you are no longer dreaming—you are doing."

"**Before long, you are no longer dreaming— you are doing.**"

* * * * *

▶ YOUNG & BOLD: ASIA NEWSON

When she was ten years old, Asia Newson became Detroit's youngest entrepreneur. She started **Super Business Girl**, a company that sells candles. "I'm the boss of this company!" she says. Asia likes helping others, too: "I teach people like myself how to make their own money." Asia hopes to become mayor of her hometown someday, and ultimately president of the United States. Dream big, Asia!

Hopefully you recognized a little of yourself in some of these stories, or you've seen a glimpse of the kind of person you'd like to be in the future. Maybe you've been introduced to a new career, field of study, or life goal.

Each of these women dreamed big—and more often than not, their dreams came true. The biggest hurdle in life is often our own imaginations. We have to step outside of what has been done to imagine what could be.

Chely Wright

Country singer Chely Wright was seventeen years old when she tuned in to "The Puppy Episode" on *Ellen*. She was watching TV with her father and sister at their home in Kansas. Chely remembers that after Ellen came out, her dad shut off the TV and said, "That's disgusting." Chely knew she was gay, but she hadn't come out. "It was kind of heartbreaking," remembers Chely. "I recommitted myself to never, ever, ever telling my secret." By 2005, Chely finally came out to her dad. He was 100% supportive, despite what he'd said about *Ellen*. He took Chely's shoulders, looked her straight in the eyes, and said: "I love you because you're one of the best people who God ever made." In 2010, Chely became one of the first country singers to come out publicly.

Ellen DeGeneres

Ellen DeGeneres stumbled into comedy after realizing she had a talent for making people laugh. Her big break came in 1986 when she appeared on *The Tonight Show Starring Johnny Carson*, the top late-night TV program at the time. In her act, Ellen made a "phone call to God," seeking his advice on questions like "Why are there fleas?" The act was a hit, and Johnny asked her to sit down with him. Only four men—and no women—had ever been asked to do that. Ellen's next big milestone came when she convinced the TV network ABC to give her her own show, *Ellen*. After several successful seasons, Ellen confessed a personal "big secret" to her manager: she was gay. Her manager thought her character should be, too, and that her character should "come out," meaning share with the world that she was gay. She did just that in 1997, in "The Puppy Episode." Since 2003, Ellen has mostly been seen on her daytime show. Ellen says, "I'm honest, and I think that really means something to people. I think people watch me on TV and go, **'She's telling us who she is. She's not hiding anything.'"**

Conclusion

IN THIS BOOK, YOU'VE learned about many inspiring women who made incredible things happen. They followed their hearts, worked hard, overcame obstacles, learned from their mistakes, jumped at opportunities, fought injustice, crushed stereotypes, helped others, and dreamed big dreams.

We've drawn lots of connections between the women in this book, and hopefully you can see connections among yourself and other women and girls you know. We can't wait to see where you're headed—and what you've already done.

Need more inspiration to get you going? Here are some words of wisdom:

"Take a chance. You will never regret taking a chance."

—**Valerie Jarrett** ➲ former senior advisor to President Barack Obama

"Keep proving yourself, because you're awesome."

—**Ayanna Howard** ➲ roboticist

"You dream it, you align your thoughts, you focus on nothing else but achieving that, and things fall into place."

—**Angela Ahrendts** ➲ former senior vice president of retail at Apple

"Believe in who you are. You are going to move people. Don't be afraid of the power that you have. Just go out there and let people see you."

—**Mary J. Blige** ➡ singer, songwriter, actor, philanthropist

"Be curious about everything. I'm talking about intellectual curiosity. Dig deep. Be curious. Have an insatiability to find out what's really going on."

—**Indra Nooyi** ➡ former CEO of PepsiCo

"If you push through that feeling of being scared, that feeling of taking a risk, really amazing things happen."

—**Marissa Mayer** ➡ former CEO of Yahoo!

"In order to get people's attention, you've got to blow a loud trumpet, you've got to beat the drum loudly. Nobody listens to you when you go quietly into the night."

—**Oprah Winfrey** ➡ entrepreneur

"Keep on being you, because ten years from now, we're all going to be working for you."

—**Jennifer Hyman** ➡ cofounder and CEO of Rent the Runway

Find Out More about MAKERS!

MAKERS HAS BEEN A valuable asset to students, teachers, parents, and anyone looking for inspiration or information. It's a great way to illuminate history and showcase women making an impact on contemporary society. For instance, if you are heading to Washington, DC, and want to visit the Vietnam Veterans Memorial, first watch Maya Lin talking about her creation. If you are doing a science project, you can watch Megan Smith and videos of other great women in science. Maybe you have to do a book report on a book by Alice Walker? You can watch her video and learn more about her.

For more about MAKERS, including its growing archive of women's stories (which includes many more than those featured in this book) and its multiple documentaries, check out Makers.com.

Also check out the MAKERS films, including:

MAKERS: Women Making America

MAKERS: Women in Comedy

MAKERS: Women in Hollywood

MAKERS: Women in War

MAKERS: Women in Business

MAKERS: Women in Politics

MAKERS: Women in Space

Once and for All

Keep in touch: WeAreMakersBook.com

Want to Learn and Do More?

Here are some organizations to look into.

If you're interested in sports:

girlsontherun.org: Girls on the Run groups meet regularly in small teams, and girls learn life skills through fun, engaging lessons that celebrate the joy of movement.

fullcirclesouljahs.com: Full Circle is a hip-hop dance company that was created by MAKER Ana "Rokafella" Garcia.

womenssportsfoundation.org: The Women's Sports Foundation was founded by MAKER Billie Jean King. It aims to advance the lives of girls and women through sports and physical activity.

If you're interested in politics and government:

girlsinpolitics.com: Girls in Politics organizes camps and webinars where girls ages eight to seventeen get excited about politics.

iCivics.org: iCivics was started by MAKER Sandra Day O'Connor to help people understand how government works.

emilyslist.org: Emily's List supports and helps pro-choice Democratic women candidates get elected.

offthesidelines.org: Off the Sidelines is MAKER senator Kirsten Gillibrand's call to action to encourage every woman and girl to make their voice heard on the issues they care about.

childrensdefense.org: The Children's Defense Fund helps fight for children's rights.

If you're interested in STEAM (science, technology, engineering, arts, math):

blackgirlscode.com: Black Girls Code introduces computer coding lessons to young girls from underrepresented communities.

girlswhocode.com: Founded by MAKER Reshma Saujani, Girls Who Code has programs all over the US that teach girls how to code.

girlsmakegames.com: Girls Make Games offers international summer camps and workshops to encourage girls to explore video games.

blackgirlsrock.com: Black Girls Rock is a youth empowerment and mentoring organization established to promote the arts for young women of color.

browngirlsdoinc.org: Brown Girls Do Inc. promotes diversity in the arts by providing scholarships, a mentor network, and community programs to empower young girls of color.

nyphil.org/education/learning-communities/very-young-composers: Through the Very Young Composers initiative, students create and hear their own music performed by New York Philharmonic musicians.

If you're interested in education and mentoring:

girlsforachange.org: Girls for a Change is a youth development organization that empowers black girls and other girls of color to visualize their bright futures and potential through discovery, development, and social change innovation in their communities.

mygirltalk.org: Girl Talk inspires girls to be confident leaders through peer-to-peer mentoring programs.

girlup.org: Girl Up is a global leadership development initiative, which positions girls to be leaders in the movement for gender equality.

gyrlwonder.org: Gyrl Wonder provides resources and helps girls leverage tools to accomplish their personal and professional goals, focusing on self-care, self-image, empowerment, development, and service.

shesthefirst.org: She's the First provides girls who will be first-generation high school students with funds needed to graduate.

studentleadershipnetwork.org/program/the-young-womens-leadership-schools: The Student Leadership Network's Young Women's Leadership Schools empower young people in low-income communities to access educational opportunities that prepare them to be change agents.

toolsandtiaras.org: Tools & Tiaras was created by MAKER Judaline Cassidy and encourages girls to make and build things.

If you're interested in girl-friendly media:

amysmartgirls.com: Amy Poehler's Smart Girls is a website with articles and more dedicated to helping young people cultivate their authentic selves.

If you're interested in health and wellness:

crisistextline.org: Crisis Text Line, founded by MAKER Nancy Lublin, is a free, twenty-four seven text line for people in crisis.

likeme.org: Like Me, founded by MAKER Chely Wright, is dedicated to providing education, assistance, and resources to LGBT teens and their family and friends.

prettybrowngirl.com: Pretty Brown Girl encourages self-acceptance of girls of color by cultivating their social, emotional, and intellectual well-being.

INDEX

Note: Page numbers in *italics* refer to illustrations.